Twelve Angels

THE WOMEN WHO TAUGHT ME HOW TO ACT, LIVE, AND LOVE

Dominic Chianese
Matthew Sargent

SAVIO REPVBLIC

A SAVIO REPUBLIC BOOK
An Imprint of Post Hill Press

Twelve Angels:
The Women Who Taught Me How to Act, Live, and Love
© 2018 by Dominic Chianese and Matthew Sargent
All Rights Reserved

ISBN: 978-1-64293-030-6
ISBN (eBook): 978-1-64293-031-3

Cover Design by Cody Corcoran
Interior design and composition by Greg Johnson, Textbook Perfect

posthillpress.com
New York • Nashville
posthillpress.com

Published in the United States of America

My father always said, "It's gonna be tough.
It's gonna be tough, it's gonna be tough, it's gonna be tough."

My mother knew that I needed to go ahead and just do it.

My mother understood me in some ways better than my father.

Because she knew the other part of me.

Prologue

There was so much wasted potential among the men and women in my family. The 1930s Depression-era Bronx practically demanded it. His name was Gaetano; I knew him as "Pop." Pop was a smart man, for sure. But his dreams, and the dreams of his brothers, needed to consist of less pie in the sky and more bread on the table. They all had seen visions of the American Dream in early American cinema but had to take jobs that were less creative than they might have liked. First-generation citizens who came from large, extended families were expected to forsake formal education and immediately earn their keep. My father was a master bricklayer.

And the Italian women were held back too. Definitely. No question about it. In those days, and especially in the neighborhood, women were kept strict. They couldn't even wear lipstick or nail polish. The women had a "role." My own mother could have been a pianist or a teacher, she was also very smart, but women became housewives and that was it.

There was a lot of drinking on my mother's side of the family, and I'm not sure I was ever put in a position to truly understand why. My mother never drank, but all of her sisters did. The closest of which was my Aunt Annie. She was only five years older than me and would always make all of us laugh. She had a great sense of humor, of timing. Annie would come up from Brooklyn and beat all the other kids at marbles, blessing me with the whole winner's lot. She was very loving and very, very protective. "That's my nephew!" she would proudly say. But Aunt Annie was an alcoholic, and she died young.

I can remember the feeling of loss at an early age. When the realization of my Grandfather Alexander's passing hit my mother, my father put his hand on her shoulder and somehow I understood that. There was not enough money for funeral homes, and it was customary to have the body, open and displayed, in the family's house. Even though I was forcibly accustomed to this uncomfortable practice, I still remember being particularly affected when I saw my mother's brother, Uncle Joe, in a casket. He was thirty-eight years old, and cirrhosis had shriveled him down to nothing.

Grandpa Alexander was a very intelligent man who had performed submarine service in Italy around the turn of the century and was then a chef who ran a Manhattan-based restaurant during the First World War. He was extremely capable and spoke many languages. My mother's mother, Grandma Florence, was illiterate, however. She was an older Italian woman who would just sit in the corner and keep quiet. She liked to sip her wine.

My mother was not a particularly affectionate kind of mother. She didn't reach for me. She didn't saturate me with hugs and kisses and smash me to her bosom like the stereotypical Italian mamma. Her love was conveyed through food, through the home environment, and through deep-felt caring and understanding. I could hear it in her voice. I knew she loved me.

Uncle Dick and Uncle Dinio, on my mother's and father's sides of the family respectively, wanted me to pursue dreams of dancing and professional ball. If the plan went accordingly, they would live vicariously through their nephew who "made it out." Pop always wanted me to be a schoolteacher. In Italian culture, schoolteachers were as revered as doctors and lawyers. That was his dream. He was a tough guy, and I believe he wanted me to be practical and not suffer. He was the son of an immigrant, who had given up on his own dreams. My mother had much more ambition than he did, and she had that ambition for me.

My first choice was music. When I was five or six, I would cross Southern Boulevard over to my father's parents, Grandma Francesca and Grandpa Domenico. And if I reached up hard enough, I could drop the steel, turkey-necked record needle onto their twelve-inch shellac records and the Victrola would play Caruso and John McCormack singing arias—it was beautiful. Grandpa Domenico would sit by the window and sing Neapolitan songs too. And after the big Sunday meal, everyone would play the guitars and mandolins to the key of D. I started to realize real beauty existed—all I had to do was attain it. Then, against every-thing my father knew to be true in this world, I got a violin.

A three-quarter violin was the only point of real conten-tion my father and I ever had. He did not want me to play it. He teased me about it. "What a sissy thing to do." But I dearly loved my little violin; I would go to sleep with it at night. I can still smell it next to me. Our neighbor, a kindly Jewish woman named Mrs. Freeman, knew I had restlessly begged my mother for one and she mercifully bestowed it upon us. I took lessons, which would often result in a painless barrage of switch thwacks from an imperious music instructor who actually thought there was talent in there somewhere. Pop knew what lay in wait out there.

Whereas Grandpa Domenico would take my other cousins out to fish for eels in the Hudson River or hunt for mushrooms in the park, I was always more content being the indoors grandson who would rather listen to him sing and explore music. Pop did appreciate music and the arts from time to time, but he also kept a tireless foothold in the Depression and knew this was a time of practicality, not hope. In fact, after I held a small service for my concerto dream and shelved the little three-quarter case for the last time, Pop and his brothers provided me with a different type of extracurric-ular education.

Our neighborhood, Belmont in the Bronx, was a very family-oriented, very safe, close-knit Italian neighborhood. We would walk the blocks to grade school by ourselves. But every now and then I'd see men in their twenties and thirties running down the street, carefully dodging the children who were on their way to school. Squad cars filled with plain-clothes policemen would be racing right behind because the men had been shooting dice in the streets. Schoolchildren like us, we didn't know at the time. Avoiding them was never an issue—we just assumed it was part of living, people running around like that. This was the Depression era, and people were doing what they had to do to get by.

So, just like out of a movie, Pop took me by hand and introduced me to the neighborhood. He pointed out everyone we passed. Pop would point to some guy and say, "He's a brick-layer, like me. I know him, we work together" and "There's the baker" and "There's Doctor Soscia over there…" And of course, Pop actually had a plan, because just beyond a stroll's length through the neighborhood we would go by a certain kind of coffee shop and he'd say, "Those are racketeers." He would never comment beyond that. With the same inflection he would say "He's a doctor" or "He's a baker," he said, "He's a racketeer." And I could tell these dapper men were somebody because they were dressed a little sharper, and they all had hats on. Of course, they were just as friendly as everybody else.

Under Pop's tuition, I was absorbing this newly-informed culture all around me, and I began to become more objective toward the different parts of the neighborhood and "character types." The once-present mysteriousness and peripheral fear of the local unknown wore away, and I allowed my fascination and careful, distant observance of the functional neighborhood to take hold. It all helped later on when

I would play hoodlums and tough guys because I understood their behavior patterns and attitudes so well.

My earliest inclination of how I would pursue my happiness came from a second-grade school play, when I played one of the signers of the Declaration of Independence. I was wearing white stockings and silk colonial trousers and trying to suppress the ceaseless swelling awe a young student lives as the minutes of "school at nighttime!" compound on one another. And I just stood there on stage—I didn't even have a line. I was contemplating this budding excitement and how it came to be when, within my own contemplative and observing world, I looked down at my silver-buckled shoes, then expanded my understanding to include the audience's presence, and had a moment of self-awareness: "Oh my God, this is fun! This is Heaven!"

Now I knew I had a drive. But Pop had already intervened early on to redirect it from music and, to a greater extent, arts in general. This left me with a few options: take up window-breaking with some of the more well-known rock throwers who operated on the fringes of my social circle at the time, disregard my mother's parable of the "kid who got hit riding a bike in New York City" and ride one anyway, or take the plunge and go all in on schoolwork. The choice to channel my energies did not prove difficult.

Pop had been laying brick since he was fifteen years old. He'd started so young that he was actually one of the first Italian guys from the neighborhood to do it. Back then it was all Irish guys, and they would call my father "Murphy" for fun. Pop even took it to heart and once asked my grandfather if he could change his last name to Murphy. Of course, this did not sit well with my grandfather's time-tested Italian heritage, and he got so upset that he chased Pop halfway around the block. But working like that for so long had ingrained traits like hard diligence, security, and tradition into Pop's belief system. Still, even though he never went past the eighth grade, Pop and his brothers respected education. They would always tell me, "You gotta do something with your head; you don't want to use your hands."

And I listened. Literally, right around the corner from our house was my grade school, PS 74, and I was constantly winning the gold medal of the year there for academic excellence. In this academic pursuit, I had a tremendous amount of love and encouragement from both sides of the family. I was very fortunate in this way. But my mother was musical too. She would play old Italian waltzes if a piano was nearby, and she understood what I really wanted. She would always push me because she knew I could do it. I just needed a little nudge.

Included with the duties of a PS 74 gold medal recipient was the obligatory "top three students" competition quiz before the whole school. This was actually my first experience of having the spotlight on stage, and it was a little frightening. From what I could tell, our close-knit Italian neighborhood featured more local gossip than all the mass-produced wire-taps and recorders in the world could ever keep up with, and this public grilling was huge. Reputations were on the line. The principal would look out into the school auditorium, then turn to me and say, "All right, Dominic, what's seven times fourteen?" And with amazing third-grade alacrity, I would submit, "ninety-eight." And everyone would say "Wow!" At least I had been able to trade my brief foray into violin virtuosity for the confidence-building measures of academic prowess.

But one year I didn't win. And my mother was watching me. At some point during that competition I realized that I could not remember my mother ever being at any of the other contests, but she had come to this particular one. And I wondered why. Having just experienced my first public humiliation, I humbly retreated from the public eye, looking for the auditorium exit faster than most of the ill-affected student audience. I was pretty upset about losing like that. I had won three times in a row. It was traumatic to lose, to know this spectacle of defeat. Somewhere in my lonesome sulk amongst my peers, my mother's voice cut through like a beacon of promise: "They had to give it to somebody else." She was teaching me to be secure in my mental abilities, that the only real competition is with yourself. That's when I first learned to truly ask, "Why can't I?"

My father had given me the neighborhood education, and now it was time for his youngest brother, my other Uncle Joe, to provide me with the advanced coursework. Uncle Joe was in many ways my favorite uncle. He was only fifteen years older than me and wound up pulling the majority of my babysitting shifts because so. He was strong, wild, and rebellious. I really looked up to him.

Uncle Joe's first lesson in street survival involved a particularly scary evening for me where he lined up all the neighborhood kids in the yard outside of my grandparents' apartment building and had me determine which one, should needs be, I could take. He would point to each member of this anxious and unsure motley crew and ask the eternal question, "Can you beat 'em up?" For this profound piece of information, I was allotted three passing answers: yeah, oh yeah, and no. But if I answered, "Well, I don't know," as I might do with a kid twice my size, then Uncle Joe just knew that I was exposing a notion of doubt that was sure to be exploited on the streets of our quaint, family-oriented Italian neighborhood. Much to my chagrin and not so much Uncle Joe's, Victor Dragotti, of said crew, was twice my size.

During the first few minutes of the Uncle Joe-sponsored fight with Victor the next day, I remember thinking, "This is kind of fun." Fun, in the sense that Victor's older brother stepped in to break it up before I could get pummeled into my second public humiliation. I actually did not like doing it in the long run. I was never really a fighting kind of kid. But that's what many boys did, and Uncle Joe thought I had to learn. It was his way of looking out for me and teaching me to stand my ground. Having survived Uncle Joe's first lesson, I was ready for the extended curriculum: a lesson that would later severely haunt me and be hard to shake.

When Uncle Joe was younger, he landed the coveted teenage vocation of Bronx Park worker. This afforded him the opportunities to interact with a wide variety of clientele—specifically, girls. And since the Bronx Park was a quick jaunt down the street from my house, I was afforded the opportunity to witness these interactions. Most of the time Uncle Joe worked with the pony rides and children. But when he pulled soda jerk duty, Uncle Joe was instantly transformed into man's gift to women. How could girls not go for such great lines as "May I hump you" instead of saying "May I help you"? And of course, for some reason, he would always draw the one girl who would be offended. She would decry, "What!?" And Uncle Joe, realizing his intended object of affection may not yet be ready for his refined suavity, would reply, "Would you like a soda?" while surveying the current customer base for the next potentially lucky future mate. Uncle Joe was teaching me to "love 'em and leave 'em," and I devastatingly learned this lesson.

At twenty-two years of age, Uncle Joe was still working out the kinks. These kinks often took the form of wild, spirited rebellion. The thing about Uncle Joe was that he was not a terribly big guy—he was only a hundred sixty pounds or so, and never really looking for trouble—but he was tough. Somehow, he ended up in an altercation with the guy who ran the little rowboats at the Bronx Park and the police were called. Three people were thrown into the lake that day, and they were all cops. Incidentally, this landed Uncle Joe in court.

Grandma Francesca went before the judge to plead, in her thick and elderly Italian accent, "Please don't put my son in jail. He's a good boy." And the judge replied, "Well, yeah, but he threw three policemen in the lake. He's in trouble. Either he joins the National Guard or he's going to reform school, or he's going away." So Uncle Joe joined the National Guard. Then he volunteered for the army. Then, America entered World War II and Uncle Joe became a paratrooper.

During the war years, the Italians in the neighborhood were very loyal to America. The fact that Italy was on the wrong side was not talked about in the household, but I'm sure the feelings ran deep. Grandpa Domenico had been born under Italy's king, Vittorio Emanuele, and felt an atavistic allegiance until he later realized Mussolini was going to bring Italy to ruin. His sons, my Uncles Dinio—who would go on to win a Silver Star for saving a man's life—and Joe, were now both fighting against his home country, and I know he felt bad about that. It was a time of crying and desperate introspection for many, and I began to realize this model of discordant duality between humanity and idealism which were rarely on the same path.

Though it was also a time of heavy prayer, my family was never very religious in the traditional sense. The men in the family hardly ever attended Sunday Mass. They respected the Church and feared it in a superstitious sort of way, but they never really trusted the priesthood. Pop would tell me, "When you really need something, priests won't give it to you." He thought of them as moochers operating within the religion. But Pop never disrespected the religion itself. He would always light candles and didn't mind that my mother kept a saint in the house. And my mother never insisted on going to church either. She was born here and behaved much more like an American woman than an old-school Italian. We were not devout Catholics, but I did grow up learning the respect part of the Church, and I enjoyed it in the ritualistic sense.

The only time I went to Catholic school was for the brief period we lived in Washington, DC. Being thirty-four years old and having two children, my father had avoided the draft and temporarily relocated us to Silver Spring, Maryland, for brick-work. New York bricklaying had dried up and all the bricklayers had moved down to the Washington, DC, suburb where the work was. They practically built that place from the ground up.

As soon as we arrived, I immediately realized that New York public schools were much further ahead than Washington, DC's, and I breezed through the classes. I was so far ahead of the other students' course of study that my parents took me out of the public school and enrolled me in Saint Martin of Tours Catholic School. Though I really looked up to Father Miltonberger and developed an affinity for intermural basketball, constantly taking orders was not my thing. Unlike within the Church itself, I was no longer able to simply exist in the "crowd"; my specific actions were now under constant scrutiny and had to be accounted for. I was a little unnerved because I was not always sure about what I was supposed to be doing. I used to cheat at prayers by speaking so fast that no one could really tell what I was saying.

Washington was a much more wide-open area than New York, and I was no longer protected by the confines of the old Italian neighborhood. I was walking down the street one afternoon when another boy said to me, "What's your name?" I replied "Dominic," and he punched me right in the nose. I'll never forget that. His father was holding his hand the whole time. I asked his father, "What the heck did he punch me for?" and they just walked away. I had kind of known that my father and grandfather had a harder time when their generations were coming up in America, but my generation of Italian Americans was pretty well assimilated. Emotions and tensions were still running deep all over the country, and people were confused in their search for meaning and identity. It was the first time I really experienced prejudice.

I had made some friends while in Washington, and when the doldrums of uniformed education would permit, we would play softball after school. They would call me "DiMagg" because I hailed from the baseball mecca of New York. Once when we were playing, a couple of my friends, who were African American, decided to ask, "Are you white or black?" And as the tears stemming from this new and confusing question began to pour down the cheeks of her dark, olive complexion, all I could think of in this rawest of moments was to answer with the closest universal truth I could reach for: "No, she's my sister."

My sister Frances was two years younger than I was, and because girls and especially Italian girls were raised strictly and regimented, our lives were not always closely intersected. I was given freedoms she was not. But we were close when we could be, particularly early on. We would compete to see who could name the capitals of all forty-eight states. She would follow me around sometimes, and I seem to remember her often "being there." I once showed another boy my pocketknife and his father instantly hit hysteria and tried to jump me. He thought I was going to harm his boy. The man later apologized for being aggressive, but Frances had seen the whole thing and was bawling terribly at the site of a grown man raising up against her older brother. We had our differences of opinion, but there was no question that my sister loved me.

One freedom I could enjoy over my sister was the ability to get a job. Though I was still young, I was offered the opportunity to carry out a newspaper route. So I asked Pop if I could take this route and he didn't say I was too young or anything, just "How much will it pay you?" And I told him the weekly bacon brought in would summate to the grand total of one dollar. Somehow, Pop did not see this as quite enough for a week's worth of work. Integrity and respect were very important to my father, and this was his way of teaching me not to sell myself short—an important lesson that I thankfully was given the opportunity to learn. I do not know if my sister would have taken the same path had she been given the same opportunities to learn life lessons as these, but I do know that she was not given the same opportunities to learn them.

Pop also taught me my first example of compassion to others. After we moved back to New York, Pop secured an "essential" position with Western Electric during the wartime, then quickly ascended the ranks of bricklaying as the industry began to flourish. He became a foreman, and if somebody was sick he made sure they got paid. One time a worker did fall ill, so he took me with him to pay the worker—in Harlem.

At the time, many parts of Harlem were heavily segregated, and Harlem as a whole was not considered generally safe. As we made the unlikely venture through a predominantly black neighborhood, I realized that my father was not afraid of peoples' conventions. And after giving this appreciative worker his pay, I realized my father was a very sensitive man. I never heard him speak badly about anyone. One of the only times I saw him almost cry was when he had to fire a brick-layer. He had a soft heart.

As well as Pop knew what I needed, my mother knew even better. My father knew my mind was scattered, that I didn't have direction. Direction was important to Pop; he had started bricklaying as a teenager and had ridden out the Depression. My mother knew that I was a timid kid and in some way needed the temerity to go forward, because she also knew I had talent. She knew. She knew her son better than anybody. Mothers do. And so, under the premise that it was a modern staple for a household and my mother's own musical influence, we got a piano.

Though we did not have a lot of money, Pop was now doing relatively all right and when we moved back to the Bronx in 1943, we were able to get a bigger apartment on Prospect Avenue. This also afforded my parents the spatial opportunity to have a piano, which was commonplace. They kept the piano in a little alcove by three bay windows in the living room, and I would tinker with it for hours.

Frances was very intelligent and she quickly learned to read music and play, often accompanying me as I unsuccessfully tried to imitate the records I knew. For some reason, even though I had such an early love for music and was almost magnetized by the piano, I never took lessons. I would just explore the keys and range for hours on end. I'm not sure it was the best thing, but it must have been the artist in me that wanted to do things in my own organic way.

There was now a musical presence in our household that was unshakeable. We lived with music. And I really believe that the piano created and fostered a positive binding throughout our home. One evening, we had an electrical fire and my mother quickly called the firemen. Pop was alerted too, and he came running home from work, arriving about the same time as the firemen. When he saw them running up the stairs, he darted after. It was understood, especially then, that the firemen were probably going to have to wreck things in order to stop the fire from spreading. And as the firemen were going in, Pop yelled over their shoulders, "Listen, you guys, get rid of the fire, but don't touch the piano!"

Other than the small fire, of which all pianos survived and were accounted for, life was fairly good. My sister and I had both applied for entry to Bronx Science High School— the prestigious educational destination for the Bronx's most erudite hard knocks—and were living the carefree junior high life of two children who were fortunate enough to have both parents stateside during wartime. The plan was sudden and clear: just sit back, relax, and envision parlance with the Bronx's high school upper crust while accumulating junior high breaks like notches in the belt. It was smooth sailing until the Christmas "break" of 1944.

It turns out that sometimes when children are cautioned "not to do something," there is, in fact, a reason. What's more, it would seem, is that there are situations that truly warrant guidance. So when you and your cousin Carmine blatantly ignore a warning to "not go down the hill at Van Cortlandt Park," and you do, and it sends Carmine flying through an iron fence and wraps your left leg up so bad in torn iron that it completely shatters your femur, you can't really say you weren't warned.

I was hospitalized for so long that my entry to Bronx Science was delayed because I lost a term. Thank goodness Carmine initially hit the fence with enough force to go clean through with only a scratch. The accident ended up being a turning point in my life. I spent four months in Fordham Hospital, which was severely understaffed because of the war. Subsequently, I was an "experiment" in medical procedure: it was the first time they had pulled a wire through somebody's heel bone and they didn't get the traction right, so I have a scar and my leg never bent back all the way. More importantly, it was a period in my life of real growth.

When you are in the hospital you find out quickly who loves you. All of my family came to see me: Pop, my mother, Frances, my uncles, and my grandparents. Grandma Francesca would kiss my cast and everyone in the ward would break out laughing. They knew I was going to get well then. There were two guys in the ward with me who were more or less homeless and they would always say, "Here comes your family again!" Mr. Sabatini from Argentina was in the bed next to me, and they were all very sweet to this thirteen-year-old who had just experienced a really bad leg break. Everybody was very supportive in this understaffed and undersupplied wartime hospital, and I began to realize that visits in a hospital setting not only affect the patient but positively impact the visitors as well.

While I was in the hospital I did a lot of reading. It was the first time in my life that I really read newspapers, and I learned a lot about the advances and progresses of the Second World War. I read about President Roosevelt dying. And when we would listen to the war reports on the radio at night, people would cry throughout the hospital because they were waiting for their husbands and sweethearts to come home. In these ways, I began to further observe and understand human nature and how things were connected and worked in the world.

At the same time, because the break in my leg was so severe, I started to truly let go of this dream I had kept on the back burner that I might try and pursue professional sports. My Uncle Dinio had coached me and planted this idea of playing pro ball—and I was a pretty good ballplayer—so I had always held this idea of a "backup" career, which, kept boiling, had prevented me from pursuing other areas more wholeheartedly. With the inability to run at full stride now, I could understandably abandon sports endeavors and more keenly lock in my focus.

Wanting to seek out new perspectives—and having become accustomed to the wide-open spaces of living in DC—I ended up spending most of my time at my grandparents' more spacious block in Kingsbridge when I returned from the hospital. I made a lot of friends there; we were a real mixture of ethnicities too—Irish, Jewish, Italian, and German. There was also an Armenian boy and a French Canadian. Even though we came from all different backgrounds, we were really just a group of kids playing on Fort Independence Street. And on August 15, 1945, I hobbled on my crutches and into the street to join everybody celebrating the end of the war.

There was stability. There was peace. My nights would be filled with watching Grandpa Domenico puffing his De Nobili cigars in the windowsill—we called them "the guinea stinkers"—and singing Neapolitan songs out to someone and somewhere we obviously could not see. And when his heart was filled, or emptied, depending how you looked at it, he would retire to all-night card games with Pop and his friends. There was Boss and Underboss, which came from southern Italy, and a partner game, Briscola, which gave the winners command of the wine.

It was wonderful to watch the dynamics of it, how the players interacted with each other. There would be these little arguments: "You played the wrong cards, stupid!"

"Well, if you had—"

"If!? If my aunt had a beard, she'd be my uncle!" They said funny things like that. Great lines. I always liked to watch older people because I would learn from them. Some of the younger people would talk about clothes and their newest acquisitions we would sure enough see, and I really didn't care about that. I cared about people's dynamics. Sometimes through my own volition and sometimes not, I had learned to sharpen my observational skills, and I appreciated the value of relationships and interaction.

As much as I had learned to observe older people and dynamics, a new area had recently developed in my life that I was not prepared for and had no experience in valuing: girls. Sometimes my friends and I would go to the Friday night Catholic school dances where the boys would sit on one side and the girls on the other. Once in a while, I would somehow get the nerve up and actually ask a girl to dance. I hated that walk over—at least pirates knew the outcome of walking the plank. If I got turned down once, that was it; I'd go home. I was very shy with girls. But the teenage years were times of bravado, and we all made up stories of conquest that gave new meaning to the word "baloney."

And when Uncle Joe came back from the war, he floated a tale of his own. He used to send me paratrooper jackets while he was enlisted. I was fourteen and had what my friends and I figured to be wartime contraband—I was so cool. Then, when Joe got back, he would back the jacket up with wartime stories. One that stood out was the song he would sing when he would jump out of the plane: *"On the dummy line, on the dummy line, rain or shine I'll pay my fine, I'll pay my fine, rain or shine...on the dummy line."*

I had the jacket *and* I knew the song: in my circle, I was practically untouchable.

So many years later, when Uncle Joe's health was failing from cirrhosis of the liver, I went to see him because everyone in my family thought the end was near. Uncle Joe took one look at my downtrodden face and said, "Don't worry, I'm not gonna die. I'll live another ten years." And he did too, in fact. He was a hard worker and a heavy drinker. He had worked hard all throughout the time he was a kid and shoveled snow as part of the WPA, the Works Progress Administration, during the Depression, up through his enlistment in the war, and into bricklaying several years after that, and he would drink cases of beer and not be affected. He never staggered. He just worked hard, drank, and sweated it out. Like I said, Uncle Joe was tough.

"But," Uncle Joe said, "just in case, I have a confession to make."

I innocently asked, "What do you mean, Uncle Joe? What kind of confession?"

"You remember that song about the dummy line I told you we sang when we jumped out of planes?"

"Yeah…"

"Well I never sang that jumping out of an airplane."

I had put stock into this specific image of war heroes singing and jumping out of planes, marching to victory with the soundtrack I knew:

"What do you mean 'you never sang it then,' *on the dummy line?*"

Uncle Joe mulled it over, then quietly murmured, "We used to sing it when I was shoveling snow for the WPA." I realized later that Uncle Joe had combined the events to give me confidence with my peers and to give me something to look up to with elements of song—because he knew I liked singing. He was always supportive, always there. I would see him throughout the neighborhood when I was struggling, and he would always offer me money and whatever I needed. I couldn't get away without him sticking a five- or ten-dollar bill in my pocket. Even when he was dying, this time for real, he said, "Do you need any money?" And the last time I saw him physically able to stand up was at the American Legion post in Haverstraw, New York, when he pulled himself up on his two walking sticks and was grinning ear to ear because I had just performed and explained the story of "On the Dummy Line."

My family was always supportive like that. I couldn't have done it without my family. Or my friends, as I found out later. They help you along the way. But as much as I needed their help and support, family and friends can only do so much. The war had ended, but mine was just beginning. What I needed was something more.

Renowned psychiatrist Carl Jung talked about how there's a woman who's part of your soul. And I can look back and see that there were situations I was part of that could be very challenging, but were ultimately helping me to grow. And behind those situations was a real love, as Jung said, "Like an angel's."

Chapter 1

ELEANOR

Geraldine Potashman was the dynamite Jewish knockout that I needed. Frank Sinatra had been singing "I've got a crush on you," and I was inclined to think so. There were rumors that heavenly creatures such as her, whose every known detail was day-traded amongst us male conquistadors like quickly evolving stock, did in fact live in proximity to our junior high. Not to let this valuable networked intel on this little-known Ava Gardner twin go unrealized, I decided to check it out.

Five blocks outside of your own neighborhood is nothing for a teen who's already figured out love. Meeting a girl's mother, that was another.

"What's your name?"

"Dominic."

"Are you Jewish?"

"No, I'm Italian."

And as I was walking home, having risen to the challenge and absolutely not even beginning to have met it, I started to think that maybe there was a little more to what Frank had been saying. So I decided to do what any sex-starved, pre-*Playboy* 1940s teenager who'd better not even begin to think about sex would do: I took up horse betting.

Joe Bosalino and I were down to our last two dollars. We had blown through twenty dollars of misguided teenage angst and when we looked around at all the fine patrons of New York's Jamaica track, we knew our manhood could very well be on the line. Go, Caliper, go. And Caliper did—winning our fate-deciding race in a photo finish. This, of course, meant going double or nothing the next week, funded by Joan Casserly's typewriter.

Joan and I would talk about things like, "Can I hock your typewriter because I know a sure thing?" then make out. This was my first time "experimenting," and if it were to receive a rating, it would have been "PG"—for Please Go away, this is lame. The sexual mores of the late '40s and '50s were much different than today, as far as the openness of sex. Women were covered up most of the time. There was a sense of modesty. This probably led me to believe it was all "harmless," though it seemed that Joan's feelings for me ran much deeper than mine did for her.

Something was taking place that made me uncomfortable. This closeness of affection, I didn't really know it. And when you are staking your confidence in every hard-fought step toward maturation, the unknown can be very scary indeed. Still, the bottomless hormonal aggression raged on. So, drowning myself in advanced make-out sessions, I poked my head up for air one day and told Joan the only reasonable thing a teenager can muster up in an otherwise "perfect situation" like this: "I was going to die."

There was a Chinese cleaners in the neighborhood owned by a guy called "Thursday" because that's all he would say when you asked about your clothes. Joan enjoyed a sterling reputation amongst us neighborhood young gentlemen, and when my good friend Pete Dean heard about my "devastating news" and subsequent need to understandingly end things with Joan, he put me through the plate-glass window of Thursday's shop.

I'll never forget that night. The window came down like a guillotine and barely missed me. But Pete made his point. It was a terrible thing to say, especially when word would travel fast. I knew things with Joan were not going anywhere—I just wanted to experiment. There was no way I was going to get committed in a relationship; though, at the time, doing so at a young age was widely accepted and in many cases preferred. Joan fell in love with me, and I may have hurt her. But I knew that I was not ready yet. My passions were just now awakening and I didn't want to be tied down. Joan had shown me that there was more than just the physical, but I had to learn how to value intimacy.

Grandpa Domenico and Pop were always against bets. My father had a lot of aphorisms that summed up his views of life, and most of them tended to be about money or betrayal. "You never win when you want to," my father would say about gambling. So, with mounting pressure that the house horseracing built could cave at any second, and after getting Joan her typewriter back, my brief foray into cheap thrills had come to an end. At least for the time being.

Eliminating vices one by one freed me up to expand my mind. I became enamored with the arts, specifically books and music. My parents kept a small bookcase with an even smaller amount of books. There was *Audels Masons and Builders Guide* for Pop; there was *Erotikon*, which featured a naked woman on the inside and served as my always-accessible but never-actually-performed "talk"—teaching me everything I didn't need to know; and there was Mark Twain. I would often reach for Twain. It was probably the first serious literature I read outside of school, at a time when academics and assigned reading were not high on my "to do in life ever" list. Through the delicately woven tales, I was developing an awareness and regard for story and character; and ultimately performance.

Along with the piano in our now larger apartment, my family had gotten our own Victrola. Now, our home was filled with Bing Crosby, Al Jolson, and Russ Columbo. The sweet, high tenor of Russ Columbo would swamp our open-windowed apartment at night. I loved it. I would imitate them. And because I was still establishing my "stage presence," sometimes when no one was looking, I would get on my knees and sing like Jolson.

The one performer who really stood out for my friends and me was Nat King Cole. We would hang out on the street corners in the Bronx and the minute a new Nat King Cole song came out, we knew about it. Later, when I heard "Unforgettable," it really was unforgettable. He was just a great singer. And that was the thing. With radio becoming as prominent as it was, that was where it was at for stardom. Before television came along, if you could croon, you were in. Sounding smooth was everything, and it was every boy's dream.

I had started to develop this idea of who I was and what I wanted to do. Even though I had done very well in arithmetic at PS 74, the successful transference of those skills to science and more advanced algebra at Bronx Science High School did not go as I had envisioned. Whereas Frances, who also went to Bronx Science, received very high marks, I was floundering on life support. I just was not interested in these more technical subjects. I couldn't bring myself to make the undeviating investment they required. One of my English teachers would ask me, "What's wrong?" and I didn't know exactly how to answer. I knew I was smart—it's just that I was searching for this deeper emotional core that I now knew existed. I would use any free study periods I had to go across the street and listen to Frank Sinatra on the candy store jukebox. I was driven by the arts.

But, just to cover all my bases, literally, I thought I would give one last try at athletics, so I went out for school baseball. Though I could not necessarily run at full speed due to my previous coming together of sled and iron fence, I could still actively compete at a high school level. However, coach John McGrath did not see it that way. In fact, his career plan for me involved the bench, more bench, and finally, when we were once losing 26-0 to Taft High School, allowing me to pinch-hit in the bottom of the ninth. Naturally, with my whole season on the line and what seemed to be the final dashing of a sports-fueled life plan, I swung for the fences. Tellingly, for me at least, the final score that day was 26–0.

My own personal scorekeeping seemed to be tallying as follows: flunking out in small, crush-based, would-be relationships, check; flunking out in subjects that were actually listed in the name of the school I had personally chosen to attend, check; flunking out even when the game was nowhere near on the line...I began to see a pattern forming. So I did what any self-denying, self-respecting artist finally does: I pursued my art.

The Bronx Science High School choir changed my life. When I joined, my voice had already turned and I now had a nice, deep baritone. My good friend Harvey Margolin and two other guys formed a quartet within the choir and we would harmonize. We would perform and be singing "*If I had my way dear, forever we'd be...*" and I would have the part "*just for you.*" And they'd go "*youuu.*" And I'd sing "*just for you.*" And the audience would go crazy. That was my first experience getting a tremendous applause, even if I was part of the group. Occasionally, I would get a personal compliment after a show like, "What a voice you've got!" and "You have a real smooth voice"; and even though I didn't quite believe it, I'd be over the moon.

And life was good. So what if I didn't pursue sports? So what if I hadn't lived up to the ideal lady's man we all bragged to each other that we were? Who needs that "small stuff" anyway when you've got singing, when you've got success? I was finally settling into something that felt good—that I was good at. We had been rehearsing in music class and I had been hearing all types of voices warming up, practicing verse, and harmonizing. And there seemed to be this soprano voice that started to stand out. And the more I focused in on it, the more it stood out. So, it was about this time that I was selectively listening when I realized that there actually was no time anymore, and it was just me and this voice. And beauty. Her name was Eleanor. Dear Lord, her name was Eleanor.

How could this be? How could I not have been told? Was the world really this capable of taking everything good, and pure, and right and giving her a name to be called by? And I fought what I knew to be true while her dirty blonde bangs hung down mercifully just enough to give me something to grasp at. I skimmed the surface, then abandoned all hope, and went adrift in her ocean-blue eyes. The elevator had arrived and my only choice was to take it. It plunged mercilessly into the depths of an abandoned mine that seemed vaguely familiar. I actually reached the bottom for the first time. And there was a canary, and its song was so just, so true, that whatever inevitability the canary's song carried with it paled in comparison to the damage that had already been done.

Eleanor performed "*Un bel dì vedremo*" from *Madame Butterfly* to make sure there was no more of me left to give. It was gorgeous. She truly had the voice of a shining angel. Her parents would take me with them when they went as a family to Greenwood Lake. They liked me and took care of me, and my heart existed in its weakened teenage condition that was only preserved by her love. Nobody could see this thing inside of me that had stolen my sense of being. To Pop and my mother, I was still Dominic. So I continued on in a perfunctory manner while I deconstructed on the inside. And it was glorious.

I went with it. I allowed myself to expand creatively and culturally. The drama department at Bronx Science was small, but I managed to finagle a few Shakespeare readings out of them. Pop and Uncle Dinio took me to see the debut of future legend Jackie Robinson when he played for the Brooklyn Dodgers in 1947. The crowd was so packed for this "unproven" groundbreaker that we had to stand the whole time. Jackie stole a few bases and the crowd went nuts. It was a wonderful day, and I knew something big had happened. I also saw Frank Sinatra at the Paramount Theatre. He came out with a brown jacket, white shirt, and green tie. I immediately identified with him because he was who I wanted to be and he was skinny, like me. My friend Bobby McKenna was there, and when he asked why everyone in the crowd was hysterical, the girl next to him overheard and smacked him with a bouquet of flowers! And in 1947, India's first prime minister, Jawaharlal Nehru, visited our school.

Just before I graduated Bronx Science, I had this feeling that I was just sick of it. I had this wonderful girl; I could sense the promise of my passions on the horizons—everything was in order in my life except that I had no actual control. I was fed up with sitting through chemistry, sitting through physics, and sitting through algebra—"sitting" being the key word because I barely got out of there alive. Emotions were now completely dictating my actions, and I needed release. My parents had not finished formal education past junior high, and I had learned perseverance and discipline from Pop with his bricklaying and Grandpa Domenico's stone-masonry, so I overcame my sledding accident with stacked, "fulfilled" credits and invoked exit's motivating compact to graduate early at seventeen. And when I thankfully finished Bronx Science in 1948 and could take a step back and finally breathe, I was able to see that my exposure to the required vigor of science and engineering would serve me in my own pursuits. Nothing without hard work would be accomplished.

The small Italian neighborhood suddenly seemed much smaller. I felt like if I walked the perimeter enough, I could burst it at the seams. And in my current state of "unbridled passions," it was all or nothing. So I decided I would immediately join the Merchant Marine and see the world. Eleanor would understand—how couldn't she? America had won the war and now it was time for "soldiers" like me to traverse these tamed lands and keep a girl to come home to. At least that was how I saw it. My parents, not so much. Since I was under eighteen at the time, I needed my parents' permission to join up. That ended that.

Next up: radio school. I had gleaned a newspaper ad for a radio school down in Times Square, and my parents had known I had this knack for singing from the Bronx Science choir, so Pop went down there with me and put down a hundred dollars of his hard-earned money for me to take some classes. Pop knew I had a voice and that I was a good communicator—and he had always exhibited an appreciation of intelligent communication through his extremely stylized handwritten notes—yet he still wanted me to pursue the highly regarded career of Italian schoolteacher and hold a steady job. I know my mother talked him into taking me down there.

After a few of the classes, I could tell that something was off. It wasn't an "academic" atmosphere. For starters, when we had initially signed up, it was just some guy sitting at a jerry-rigged desk in a barren room. Plus the classes were slow, and the content didn't keep pace. I could see that I might be able to squeeze *something* out if I kept at it down to the very last drop, but the end result would nowhere near compensate Pop laying out that sweat-soaked cash. That ended that.

In between my short-lived endeavors, I had developed a knack for rolling barrel pins up at the Bronx's local 238th Street bowling alley. I would play against older guys and—due to my multiplying free time—got to be pretty good. Grandpa Domenico would poke his head in the door every now and then to make sure that the one-dollar pot we would play for would stay at just that. He knew that the love of money, and especially fast money, could dead-end quick. Grandpa taught me by "being"; he never said "don't."

Bobby McKenna, who had taken roses to the dome over questioning Frank Sinatra, had his father help me land my first real job. His father was a security guard down on Wall Street and helped get me a glorified clerk position with Morgan Stanley. Inspired by Pop's careful notation, I would actually deliver personally handcrafted messages to Henry S. Morgan and partners of the firm. Less of Pop's inspiration and more of my own, when the phone rang I would answer it, "Yeah? It's me," and the woman who supervised the clerks would correct with: "You have to say 'It is *I*.'" I'd wear a suit and tie and since lunches were on the house, I'd eat ice cream and chocolate pudding every day. This was the life.

But Eleanor wanted more. She wanted more for me, more for her—she could tell I was just drifting. I had been riding a false wave of security, knowing that Eleanor was obliged to be here while I sampled the many opportunities this world had to offer; at least, New York City, that is. She was a year behind me and when we danced at her senior prom that year, we had never been closer and further apart. She had correctly identified my lack of direction. I didn't really want to go straight to college and sit in another classroom, and I didn't want to commit to anything outside of what felt "good." I had seen that my position at Morgan Stanley was going nowhere and actually had my mother call them up to cover me not going in. I thought a good thing was getting better when Eleanor told me she was enrolling in nursing school upstate.

This was perfect. I no longer would have to account face-to-face for trying and quitting a new plan every few months, and by the time she was finished with nursing school, I would have everything figured out and in order for our new life. So, naturally, with Eleanor off to school for a year and myself now being of proper age, I enlisted in the U.S. Marine Reserve.

I served at Camp Lejeune, North Carolina, and did maneuvers on Myrtle Beach. They made me number one gunner on the mortar because they figured a science-based high school guy was smart. I was a hero-for-the-day among the recruits once when I reached into the gun barrel to retrieve a misfire—though it was neither brains nor brawn shown ultimately after they admitted it wasn't a real shell. They didn't want us rookies to blow ourselves up, and we didn't half know the difference anyway.

And the next day's test didn't find rooks the much wiser. I was given guard duty and a dummy rifle and told to patrol a mapped-out path in the woods of North Carolina. Now this dummy rifle, it was really just a piece of stick. And I'm from the Bronx, so it's not all "Hansel and Gretel" through the woods for me on a regular basis back in New York. I'm deep down the footpath in the pitch-black nighttime and I hear this *grrrrrrr*. And it starts to rain. I figure I could either let the rain marinate me for what I knew to be a vicious grizzly definitely hiding behind the closest tree, or I could hightail an about-face and risk doubling my "false courage" reputation I had built up from the day before. The captain back at camp upheld my reputation's good standing:

"How come you're not on guard duty!? If this were the regulars, you'd be shot!"

Of course, I was too exasperated to discern exaggerations. The captain asked how old I was and where I was from, and luckily my faraway tales of brick and mortar sufficiently mitigated him down to a "get back out there with your poncho on—it's raining." I assumed I'd let the bear work its part of the woods this time.

I also had a childhood problem resurface when I was down at Camp Lejeune. I wet the bed all through my earlier years, up until my late teens. And it wasn't really known or an embarrassment until I got into the Marine Reserve, and it happened again. This was it. I thought it was third-times-the-charm and they were going to laugh me all the way back to the Bronx. But the sergeant was understanding. "Hey, don't worry about it. A lot of people wet the bed," he allayed. It might have been a physical thing or it could have been a stress thing, I don't know. But what I could not get over was this compassion I was shown for what I perceived to potentially be a very humiliating situation.

When I got back from my stint that summer, I had two things waiting for me: bricklaying, on account of my still lack of direction, and a letter from Eleanor. She wrote, "Maybe intelligence is kind of knowing something is true even before you have the experience of it." I could not allow myself to fully absorb the meaning. All I could think of was to hurry up and get on some kind of track so that when we were rejoined she could see that I had made strides—for her, for me, for us. It was time to refocus. It was time for singing lessons.

Marguerite Haymes loved music and her passion for it was so strong. She was probably in her fifties at that time, and she was a little dramatic-looking. I was in awe of her. I would sit at the piano with her and she would explain, "It's all about phrasing. When you come to words with two syllables, just go right through it. Like the words 'serving' and 'coffee.' You don't say 'serrrrrrrrr-viiiiiing coffffffffffff-eeeeeeee.' You go 'serving coffee.' But when you get to a three-syllable word, you play with it. 'Wonderful' has three syllables, so you say 'serving coffee is woooooooon-derrrrrrrrrr-fuuuuuuuul' but you don't say 'serrrrrrrrr-viiiiiing coffffffffff-eeeeeeee is wonderful.'" And this technique really worked. She was a great teacher and had a good voice; and interestingly enough, she studied yoga way before it became big. Above all, though, she encouraged me.

I spent my days laying brick with Pop. I had to join the union, and it was run strong. Everybody raised their hands when they were supposed to. The meetings were run like a dictatorship: a room full of "ayes." I got paid one dollar and ten cents an hour, which was a lot for an apprentice. It was grueling heat that August of '49 and Pop had me punch a trowel through mortar for hours when I first started so I could build up strength. He still wanted me to use my mind and get a college degree, but I just wasn't ready for another round of classroom exercises. In a way, though, I think Pop was proud to have me working alongside him that summer.

I also managed to hook up with this guy who would bring singers into the Bronx nightclubs. He'd let me tag along and I'd wait until 1:30 in the morning for a chance to get up and sing. The accompanist would start the song and my knees would be trembling, but I knew I had to get through it. I had raw talent—I could see that—but I had not yet figured out how to perform publicly. I was still a little afraid to actually get up and do it. And one time after a late, late performance, I was walking out and somebody grabbed my arm, saying, "You did a good job, kid." I needed it, and it meant a lot.

And so I had managed to string together this ragtag routine of bricklaying, off and on singing lessons, and late-night performances. I really wasn't sure of what I was doing yet, but I at least knew that I wanted to keep arts on the periphery. It wasn't ideal, but it was something. And just as important, it could be something to Eleanor.

When you're in New York City, you become accustomed to the insisting cacophony that is city noise: cabs flying down alleyways blaring car horns to alert distressed walkers of "hope," the eternal truck "reverse warning chime" stemming from the truck you never actually see, overheard conversations that bring new meaning to "colorful English," dogs barking, cats meowing, mailbox latches unfastening and slamming, doors closing, windows shutting, phones ringing. The first time I really heard a phone ring was when it was followed with, "We need to talk."

The candy store on Soundview Avenue was a window to the past. I could look out from the booth and still see myself and my friends standing on the corner, combing our hair, waiting for the next Nat King Cole hit to drop. And here I was with Eleanor: her back from school, me becoming a man of the world—us, all grown up. So it really should have been no shock to me when a small tear formed below her right eye and it broke my heart. Because it was, and it did. Words had lost their relevance by then, but I remember her saying something after the fact, to the point of, "I can't see you anymore."

We had been sitting there in this little candy store booth, which had seemed like more than enough world for me up until this point. Eleanor was direct. Her parents were professional people, and they had impressed in their daughter that she and her suitor would have a profession. Eleanor was going through nursing school and that was it. And she had asked me what I was doing with my life, and I said I was going into business, thinking about Drake School, mastering the Spanish language—desperately clinging to anything that would convince her I was the bon vivant her family needed me to be. Anything but the truth: that I was still figuring things out and had no idea how to go about being a professional singer, a performer. Eleanor knew I had potential, but she was right: I was a drifter.

Vacancy seems to entail obligatory actions. So it really did not change very much when Eleanor said her goodbyes, got up, and left me pondering this purgatory of ambivalence. The teardrop had created a void through which all could have passed, much of which would have been barely detected. On the one hand she had truly went; on the other, finality was at least somewhere on the horizon. And I was caught hurting, lost somewhere in between.

I had lingering truths about myself. Everything was distant and behind. I would lay brick but I wasn't really laying brick. The sun would bear down, inducing sweat so I knew I was there, but the setting sun was like me: very far away.

The dusk was coming any minute; those surrounding were the dawn. My parents had been trying for several years to have another child, and despite many miscarriages, my mother at age forty-five gave birth to Toni Jean. Since I was old enough, the nurse questioned "Who's the father?" when Pop and I visited my five-pound sister in the hospital, and an overly proud Pop threw his weight into "*Me!*" And after weeks of nurturing, Toni Jean was fine—her loved and unexpected incandescence living proof of what might be.

And in the radiating persistence that increases with time, I began to hear promise again. The ability to express, to convey, to be light—I had seen that this was in me. It would not go away. Then, like so many times in my life when I couldn't do it on my own, a friend reached down and picked me up.

Jerry Major, a buddy of mine from the neighborhood, had also been "drifting" in and out of ventures, so we had a lot in common in that respect. We had been hanging out, talking about our misadventures and what's next; and through vigorous, then focused daydreaming and discussion, we made a pact that education was the only way for us to get out of this mess. So Jerry got his retired policeman father to give us a lift up to Champlain College in Plattsburgh, New York.

Besides the textbooks, the education was free. And even though I wasn't winning gold medals at the time, my diploma from Bronx Science was enough of a credential to get me moved to the front of acceptance. Jerry was my unofficial "guide" through the whole process. He helped me sign up for classes, learn the nuances of the beautiful northern New York campus, and showed me how to carefully stack pizza boxes around the not-so-carefully stacked laundry in our dorm room. Even though I was little homesick, I had a buddy, so I never had to say it.

I started to let my fragileness chip away, and I began to look forward to the airy, starry evenings of upstate New York. Perhaps, it was even "nice" to be away from home. And one evening soon thereafter, I was approached by the provost, who said, "Mr. *Ch-eye-an-easy*, I understand that you like to sing. Would you mind leading the freshmen cheer?" Adding, "Just remember to acknowledge everybody: the provost, the dean of students and fellow students, fellow faculty, and distinguished faculty before you do it." Then he handed me what I supposed was the "cheer book" and walked away.

It was the official freshmen welcoming night and all the freshmen were standing in line wearing sweaters, preparing to be greeted by the whole faculty and older students. There was an announcement: "And now, Dominic *Ch-eye-an-eese* is going to come up and lead the cheer." All of a sudden, I was on the auditorium stage in front of everyone. Everything came rushing back. I got nervous. I forgot the order of what I was supposed to say. But the performer in me that had never truly went away came rushing back as well.

So, clutching the mic, with my thickened Bronx enunciation, I bellowed, "Aw right, guys, let's do it!" And the whole place burst out laughing. And while they were laughing, I did even more of an impromptu cheer and brought the house down. The comedian in me came out. The more relaxed I became, the funnier I was.

The next day, I got a ton of compliments. Everybody came up to me and said, "Gee, you did a great job, Dominic." That's when I started to realize that I could really have a strong stage presence. If I let go and focused only on the performance, it was genuine. When I stripped away everything to just myself and the audience, I was alive.

I tried out and was cast as Enobarbus in the college production of *Antony and Cleopatra*. There's a speech that Enobarbus gives where he dies of a broken heart. It's a tough speech—you really need to have some life experience under your belt to give it. And giving it, all I could think about was the candy store, and how Eleanor's one tear said everything we could ever say in a lifetime. And how I fell.

There was a complete hush over the audience. They got it. Of course, since this was all taking place within my acting infancy, I was still working out a few craft specifics. When the cast had picked up my body, instead of holding me horizontally to themselves, they turned me toward the audience. This not only revealed that I had chosen to wear regular sneakers instead of Roman sandals, but that the particular pair I had chosen had a big hole in the left shoe. And since my character's death was the crux of the scene, the spotlight was on me and subsequently the hole in my shoe. This scene, which had initially won everyone over with the believability of tragic heartbreak and death, now found the audience roaring with laughter as they carried me off stage. We had "successfully" made it funny.

Champlain College was filled with World War II veterans attending classes through the GI Bill. Under the charge of the strikingly insightful glee club director, Doctor John Miller, some of these guys formed an elite a cappella group known as the Champlain College Drones. I had developed a bit of a campus reputation for singing and performance—albeit with sometimes unintended yet captivating results—and a wonderful thing happened: I was asked to join the group.

We traveled to Williams College, to Colgate, to Ivy Leagues, to women's colleges, and I was really the big man on campus then because it was considered a big deal to be in the Drones—and I was just a freshmen singing bass! Again, I began to let myself explore the arts and soak up culture. I studied under the music professor, Doctor Daniel Devezzani; I did some more Shakespeare; I was in the operetta *The Gondoliers*—my first foray into Gilbert and Sullivan. And I read Thomas Paine. For the first time, I really questioned my inherited belief system. I would think, "What is this provincialism we have down in the Bronx? In Italian culture?"

College was giving me singing; it was giving me acting—I was growing up mentally. And this time, I purely focused on the arts, on the growth. My friend Alvah Canfield, who was amongst the many veterans now attending school, would try to get me to date girls that he knew, but I wouldn't do it. And there was another girl who was European and was making it easy—her parents wanted her to be with an "educated guy"—but I just couldn't get involved. There was a void, and it couldn't be filled the same way; not now, not yet at least. My identity was being forged out of headfirst pursuit and growth, and if I stopped to look back, I knew I wouldn't be able to bear what I saw. I was still hurting from Eleanor, but I had figured out how to use that through undeterred drive.

So it was no small shock when it was announced in 1952 that Champlain College would be converting to an air force base for the Korean War. We had been promised by Governor Dewey that the school would remain open, so there was this slighted palpability all throughout the campus. It was one of the first times that I was actually politically incensed. I protested the school's closing in New York City. The college meant a lot to a lot of people, and it seemed that there was an educational system that didn't always coincide with education.

Military recruiters would appear on campus. A recruiter specifically sought me out, perhaps because I had been in the reserves. They gave me a physical and I was really scared that any day a letter would come and I'd ship out. But my sledding accident had in a way been fortuitous. Because my leg could never bend back properly, they made me 4-F: I wasn't fit for duty. Considering my reaction to the "bear" in North Carolina, I was thankful.

Champlain closed down after the spring semester in 1952, and I was headed back to New York. This, in itself, was not completely disappointing because I wanted to get into show business and the city was where the real breaks were anyway. My focus and successes while at Champlain had awoken the artist in me and for the first time in my life, I knew what I wanted. The only thing was, I didn't know how the heck to get it.

Chapter 2

CAMILLE

As soon as I got home, I wasn't pleased. I learned that my sister Frances had become engaged at eighteen years of age. It wasn't so much the idea that she had decided to get married I was against, it was the circumstances surrounding the marriage that I knew to be true.

Because it was customary of the times for women—and especially women within the Italian culture—to behave in a defined, expected way, my father had been very strict with Frances's upbringing. When she was sixteen years old and had just started dating, my father would wait up for her every single night she was out. He was very, very possessive. One time, Frances had dated a non-Italian boy, perhaps he was Jewish, and my father became concerned. Then she briefly dated another non-Italian boy and that was it for my parents.

All of my relatives got together. It was a big family meeting to determine how to re-correct my sister before she could, in their eyes, completely spiral out of control. And they nominated Joe Zimbalatti, a navy veteran and subway worker—and of course, Italian—to be Frances's life partner. I didn't necessarily doubt that they cared for each other deeply; it was that I knew how intelligent Frances was, and my family, under the premise of societal expectations and tradition, had basically pushed her duly into an arranged marriage without the option to pursue any personal interests. And Frances, having been raised so strictly and possessing such a sweet disposition as to not even begin to think about challenging societal norms, was compliant. But I also knew that Frances was smart enough to see what she was doing, and I think part of her agreed to this marriage because it was the only way to get out of the house and make a life.

Upsetting as this was to me, I was still figuring out how to make a life of my own. The dream of show business was still fresh inside me from my successes at Champlain, yet the daily trappings of real-world burdens were already forming. My sister's engagement was a sobering reminder of reality back in the Bronx, plus I needed a steady nine-to-five. So I went back to bricklaying with Pop, this time dream firmly gripped in hand. The days turned to weeks, and the weeks to months, but I wouldn't relinquish my grip solely to my trowel—knowing that this was only a temporary thing.

One morning, as mornings would so often go, I was on the bus with all of the other bricklayers, having gotten a late start on this particular day, heading out of town to build up all the newly planned garden apartments. There were about twenty of us bricklayers on the bus, and, due to seniority, I was sitting in the back, tuning out the day's task that lay ahead and deeply engrossing myself in the *New York Herald Tribune.* As I absorbed what was determined to be the news, I came across the help wanted section, which was ironic to me because that was actually what I needed. An ad stood out: "Singers Wanted: Jan Hus Theatre, 351 East 74th Street, auditions for American Savoyards Gilbert and Sullivan Company."

I remembered thinking, "Well, I did do the Gilbert and Sullivan operetta *The Gondoliers* at Champlain—and I tremendously enjoyed myself." Plus, *The Gondoliers* had been about Italian singers; so I quickly made these connections between myself and Gilbert and Sullivan. Then I thought, "Maybe I should go do this."

Usually, we would have been to the construction site by this point in the morning, but we had been running behind and had left the Bronx at 8:00 a.m., which was very late to get started on a construction job. Because of this, we were still in the city. The ad said the audition was at 10:00 a.m. I looked up. We were only ten blocks from the George Washington Bridge, the mythically irrevocable point of no return: New Jersey.

I quickly thought it over: remain as is and plan for another day of bricklaying, or pass by everyone in the crew as I made my way up the bus to ask Pop about a singing audition. Something told me it was now or never.

Pop, who had worked his way up to foreman and was now not only my father but the boss man of the entire crew, sat at the front of the bus with his arms folded. And for some reason, as I hurriedly gathered my courage and made my way up the bus, my now-pounding thoughts of *what* I was actually going to tell Pop allowed one lone voice to seep in, and I distinctly heard one bricklayer tell another, "Oh, I got four hundred dollars saved up in the bank." By the time I got to Pop, I had my tools, my lunch pail, and nothing but the truth.

"Pop, can I get off?" Standing there with all my equipment, I must have looked like I was ready to go to another site. He looked at me like I was crazy.

"What for?"

"An audition."

Pop thought for a second. "What's that?"

"For singing."

This time, there was an eternity. We must have missed 74th Street—it seemed so long. Then, and I'll never forget this:

"Okay."

So I got off at 74th Street, and the bus kept going with my old life.

When I knocked on the door of the Jan Hus Theatre, a tall, attractive blonde woman answered the door and said, "Yes, what can I do for you?"—because standing there in my bricklayer uniform with my gear, I must have looked like I was the resident plumber. I told her I was there for the audition, and she notified me that I was actually early but invited me inside.

When I went in, I immediately saw Dorothy Raedler sitting with Sally Knapp, who was the soprano lead of the company, and Rue Knapp, the male head of the company. They asked if I was a singer. I told them "yeah," and they asked if I had any experience. I told them I did *The Gondoliers*, thinking I would immediately be "in." It wasn't that easy.

"What part did you play?"

"I understudied the Duke of Plaza-Toro"—except when I said it, I said it with my Bronx accent and it came across like a hard "dook."

Dorothy Raedler quickly corrected: "You mean the *Duke*"—with what speech instructors call a "liquid U," which is kind of like a diphthong so it sounded like "Deeyouk."

"Yeah, that's what I just said"—not realizing how strong my accent was at the time.

"All right," Dorothy conceded as she passed me on to Rue for an audition. Fortunately for me, I think they must have known that talent can come from the most unlikely of places.

Rue met me on the auditioning stage and asked why I didn't bring any music. I told him that I had just seen the ad as I was on my way to a construction site and had literally hopped right off the bus. I appreciated how professional everyone had treated me up to this point, as I could have easily been dismissed for what seemed to be a thorough lack of preparedness. Rue and I settled on "Old Devil Moon" from Harburg and Lane's Broadway musical *Finian's Rainbow*. "*I look at you and suddenly…*" I began to sing. I thought back to when I had seen Frank Sinatra and emulated what I could.

When I finished the song, Dorothy came all the way down to the stage and said, "To me, you seem to be like a diamond in the rough. Can you come back tomorrow and bring some music from the show or sing something from Gilbert and Sullivan?"

So I came back the next day, sang again, and got hired. And that's when I began my career in show business.

We immediately hit the road. I got an Actors' Equity card before I did any professional acting because the Chorus Equity—which I was now a member of—had merged with the Actors' Equity Association. Though this was a standard technicality for most performers, it seemed like the big time to me. We toured for about ten months and it was a thrilling experience, getting to travel and perform with all of these wonderful actors. Everything had happened so fast that even though I was immensely enjoying the opportunity, I did also begin to miss my family and friends.

My loneliness in this exciting setting allowed me to finally do what had previously been the unbearable: I begin to think of another girl. Perhaps in some mix and need of friend, mate, and a maternal longing, I lowered my emotional barrier and filled my head with thoughts of Beatrice, an older woman in the group. She was a modest woman of the times, and the more time I spent with her and the touring cast, the more I became fixated on an "us" scenario. If I could just win her over, I thought, I would have it all.

Opening myself up just a little had revealed how raw I still was. And this drove my immediacy to replace the hurt. So I tried to move exceedingly fast with Beatrice. After all, who knew how long this tour might last? If I was going live out this ideal situation I had worked out of performing with a girl, a "family" on the side, I had to move quick. But when I went to meet her mother, she beckoned me into her car. "Beatrice is not for you, she's older," her mother said.

And there was a time soon after when I found Beatrice and Rue on break, listening to the records of famous tenors. I wasn't sure what to make of the condition: they both had tears in their eyes. Knowing something had to be wrong, I asked why they were crying. Then with slowly realizing watery eyes, they looked at each other, then at me, and Rue suggested hauntingly, "Someday you'll understand." Life might have gotten a little bigger just then, and Beatrice's mother had begun to make sense.

Rue Knapp was a true friend. He really loved me. He painted a beautiful gouache portrait of me and gave it to my mother. He always respected me and never made a pass. His love went far beyond sexuality. And when my sister Frances did marry Joe later that year, Rue taught me "Ave Maria," then accompanied me when I sang it at their wedding in the chapel. He was a very generous and understanding person, and a real mentor.

But even though I was getting to perform and live out my dream, the touring life was beginning to take its toll. This was my first professional experience and constantly being with the same group of people in new and different locations was kind of a shock to my system. I had gone from bricklaying with the neighborhood family and friends to instant performer and road warrior with great professional people—but a group that I was more or less required to be with nonetheless. The confines of this structure may have been overwhelming. I had attempted—in what I understood to be my best ability—to branch out and make a new life with Beatrice. But when that didn't work, I felt relegated to the outskirts of this world I was subjected to be in. I came to a point where I had to get away from all of it, to have some kind of release. So when I told Dorothy Raedler that I had to leave, I think she understood.

Before I left, though, I invited everyone in the cast over to my mother's house for a big lasagna dinner. And half the guys were gay, although they didn't use the term "gay" then. And many of the women in the company were gay too. There were actually only like three straight people in the whole group. This didn't really bother me so much—it was more new to me than anything—but Pop was definitely concerned. He watched how most of our dinner guests had a peculiar gait when they walked back and forth, and he worried that I was going to become like some of the guys in the company.

My mother didn't seem to care at all. She was only concerned for my happiness. But there was one particular group member, Henry, who would send me letters that could sometimes sound like love letters, and my mother would open and read them. She would say, "How come Henry's writing to you?" And I would tell her not to worry and it was harmless, just the "scene." She never made too much of a deal about it, but I always knew Henry had a crush.

Above all, my parents supported me. They could see that I was happy singing professionally and being on stage, and they began to understand what I wanted to do with my life. They could see that I believed in myself. Even if my chosen field could be less "traditional" than laying brick, both of my parents wanted me to do what made me happy. And when they saw that I could do it successfully, as with Gilbert and Sullivan, they began to really believe too.

Then what better time to begin? I had been asked by well-known booking agent Charlie Rapp to meet because he had heard that I had finished my stint with Gilbert and Sullivan and wanted to give me a job. This was it. I was moving up quick! I went over to his office in the Catskills and could barely contain my enthusiasm as we talked. But I knew if I could just weather the conversation and not do anything rash like spastically kick his desk out of sudden jubilation, or reach to shake his hand and miss by a few feet, putting an exuberant handgrip through his coffee, then everything would be set. This was my dream being gratified! There was just one last request that Charlie made: he wanted me to change my name.

It was so close, my dream. Charlie literally wanted to hand it to me. But I just couldn't take it, not like this. And it killed me. But I remembered back to when Pop asked my grandfather if he could change his name to "Murphy" and how Grandpa Domenico chased him around the block for even considering doubling back on our proud Italian heritage—and what it must have meant to forsake Grandpa's homeland. I had too much respect for my father, for my family and tradition: a respect that was impressed in our culture. So just like that, I walked out.

If I wasn't going to go out with the artists, I decided I would go to where the artists were. So I rounded up my friend Jack Freimeier and his friend Floyd, who was an ex-monk, and we got an apartment down in Greenwich Village. Now this was a particularly trendy area, especially for 1953—so much so, that my father bolted down to make sure I wasn't living a certain lifestyle that he wasn't used to.

I was cutting loose in this thriving artistic community so that's probably how it happened. I didn't really have much direction, but I was hopped up on vim and courage from my successful run with Gilbert and Sullivan and didn't really need it. Based upon my one and only success, and from my young, shortsighted appraisal, things just seemed to be falling my way. What I didn't realize was that I, in turn, could fall much, much harder.

There was a theatre scene down in the Village, and some of these playhouses were the equivalent to Off-Off-Broadway before there actually was an Off-Off-Broadway. And I had gotten into one of these slapdash productions, a musical in fact. So I had this tendency to really soar with emotion when I was involved with music, which was not a good thing in this case because there was this beautiful, voluptuous girl with curly blonde hair who was singing soprano in the cast. And

I asked her out on a date. And she sang in my ear, so it was pretty much over.

Many of the old Neapolitan songs, much like the ones my grandfather would sing out of the window on warm summer nights, are about a woman named "Carmela." My world was now drenched with a girl named Carmela, so I could relate. Somewhere between the memories of Grandpa's songs and this glorious siren down in the Village, I rode the sonic waves of love cries past wherever Grandpa had been crooning to out the window for all those years. She actually went by "Camille"; but she kept doing that thing where she would sing in my ear, so really, what's the difference? To be fair, I lasted about two months.

There was a dilemma. On the one hand, even in the "trendy art" scene, people weren't doing a whole lot of sack-hopping back then; on the other, if Camille kept being Camille—which I assumed she would be—and kept singing in my ear when I would least expect it, then I was seriously going to have to break with tradition. A toxin crept over me and I was invaded. And as I was about to forsake this crippling misery called constrained love, I gave one last thought to the structure and tradition at my foundation that had not yet been permeated. So after several weeks of intense hanging out, it came to this: "Camille, will you marry me?"

"Isn't this kind of sudden?"

"Well, what else can we do?" She mutually understood the sack-hopping thing.

"Well, all right."

I didn't know her background, and she didn't know mine. All I knew was that she was Italian American, she liquefied me on a nightly basis with her song, and that our runaway love was spearheading this newer, up-and-coming generation of artists who could prove that you can just figure it out along the way.

I got to meet most of her family for the first time when we got married in Brooklyn. It was a big wedding in a nice Catholic church and it seemed even bigger because of Camille's large family. She had a sister and several brothers, and one of her younger brothers noticed my family and said, "Hey look, they're working people like us!" Almost all of her brothers were longshoremen, and I came from a family of bricklayers, so it was true: we were all working people and maybe this was going to work out. And just to seal the deal, Camille sang "My Hero" at the wedding, and of course, I could barely move.

Camille's brother Frank—the one brother who wasn't a longshoreman—was actually a famous photographer and was instrumental in helping Camille and I get started. He helped get us our first apartment in a Jewish neighborhood on Sackman Street, and for a time we had a mezuzah on our door. Then we got another apartment in Brooklyn, and it seemed like we might have a life.

I would spend my days trying to get involved with local productions and work nights at Colonial Airlines. Here, knowing that this was absolutely temporary until I was "rediscovered," I decidedly used a different name: "Dick Chase." It was a role in a way. Since I would be answering the phones rapidly, I figured I could save time instead of talking everyone through "*Ch-eye-an-easy.*" I was "Dick Chase, nightly airline clerk to the world," and I would take airline reservations in pencil while operating a plug-in switchboard telephone bank. This was all good and well, but then "temporary" started to become "extended temporary."

I had met Camille through show business and I wanted to stay in show business. And I also had this strong sense of responsibility as a newfound "family man," but I could not shake this drive for show business. So when Camille indicated that she was fine with our extended routine of me holding a steady job with Colonial Airlines, part of that drive for show business seemed a little more diminished because this is how I had initially known Camille. And there were misgivings, because I didn't *really* know Camille, not at soul-mate depth, not yet anyway, so it came across that she was reneging on her identity as a performer too.

Although I didn't know everything about Camille, she was Italian American after all, and especially back then that said a lot about how someone, particularly a young woman, was brought up to be—what ideals and structure, to an extent, they held. Between this and Camille's performing, and heart-melting singing, I assumed I had enough of a foothold on her identity to comfortably begin a marriage. And even though Camille was settling into our now more "structured" lifestyle of me holding a steady job, I suppose, knowing her Italian upbringing, that she didn't completely catch me off guard by doing so. However, what she did next did.

After about two years of this local theatre and steady job routine, of which I had recently switched over to work at the Monrovia Port Management Company, Camille came home one night with some dresses. Now, this being New York, it was not immediately suspect that there was no accompanying retail bag—she could have easily bought them at a sidewalk sale, etc. Still, it was nighttime, and she hadn't brought an armful of clothes home before, so I asked, "Where'd you get the dresses?"

And she said, "I don't know, I just took them." And there was a pause. Then she told me at one point in her life she had received shock treatments. When Camille would sing to me, it would feel as if I could not move because, literally, it felt like all the weight was in my shoes—that I was experiencing the most impactful thing I could possibly experience at that moment and there was no reason to be anywhere else. This revelation was about ten times that.

I had no idea what to do. I called up Jack Freimeier because he seemed close by, as if that might help somehow. "Jack, what should I do?"

He told me about the Adler Clinic up on Central Park West and suggested I take Camille there so they could diagnose and treat her. It was new, but it was manageable. People made mistakes, right? Even those who initially gave her shock therapy might have been wrong in hindsight. I told myself these things as I got Camille enrolled in the clinic. She went a couple of times and I began to slowly breathe again; but then one night she didn't come home, and that's when we were finished.

For better or worse, one thing that had been instilled in me from the beginning was that the women of the family led very structured lives at home. My mother had done it, my aunts and grandmothers had done it, and my sisters were doing it. It was Italian culture: it was part of the times. There was a clearly defined line between an artistically free-spirited woman—like the many women that I began to encounter in the evolving theatre world—and a spouse who didn't come home. And those two lines never, never crossed. Especially not back then. So being that we were all Italian, we did the only right thing you can do in a situation like this. We had a big family sit-down.

And all of Camille's longshoremen brothers showed up to this big sit-down. And these guys, these longshoremen, they were rough. One guy actually showed up with a hook. I let Camille do all the talking. I had to. These guys looked like they were ready to jump at the sound of a word against their sister. My family wasn't able to get much in edgewise either. And Camille revealed a little more of herself when she started making up fictitious scenarios that had never occurred. It was pretty disconcerting to hear Camille in this unfounded manner, and, as far as I was concerned, pretty unpardonable too. But her brothers took the point of view of, "She's a good girl and you married her." They were either in denial or Camille had managed to hide her past from them also.

But I guess they eventually came around, because one day while I was working at the Monrovia Port Management Company, one of her brothers came over with annulment papers and said, "Dominic, I hate to do this, but I'm serving you with the papers. The marriage isn't going to work."

And I said, "You're telling me!" I wasn't always known as the most talkative one in the group, but right then, I could have said more.

I signed the papers, and I knew it was over—especially after seeing that side of Camille during the sit-down—but I was sick about it. I stayed in bed for a whole day. Here I was, twenty-four years old, a time when most guys my age were already settling into their careers with their families, and I had not really begun a career path. Plus now, I had annulled a marriage and was ceasing a potential family when most men were growing theirs. I had disgraced myself, my family.

This was all compounded by the lawyer I had to hire, a cousin of a cousin, who convinced me to get an annulment and let him handle the divorce aspect with the Church. But even though it was explained that Camille had deep-seated emotional issues she had hid, the Church's stance was, "You're married for life."

Pop and Uncle Joe had been very supportive throughout this time for me, telling me "Don't worry, you didn't do anything wrong." But when Pop heard that the Church wouldn't even consider an exception for me, he became irate. He blasted, "Give 'em five hundred dollars, they'll give you your annulment!"

And I had to lie to get a civil divorce too. We didn't have a "classic" reason like adultery, and hiding one's real self from a spouse wasn't going to cut it, so I had to play the bad guy and say I did not want children in order to make it official. When I was signing this decry against populating the earth that I was forced to make, I had this notion that the legal law exists somewhere below an overall moral consciousness. And if this was true, then there had to be more.

So I pulled myself together. At least I still had my port job where I would answer the phones—and I didn't even have to break out "Dick Chase" because this time the call volume gave me enough time to sound out *"Ch-eye-an-easy."* With my marriage completely dissipated, all I really had now was sitting in this little office with my boss and answering phones: clarity.

Love had come and gone, but my passion had remained. I could see that my passion and belief had tenacity. There was this thing inside me: fear, determination, anguish, a hurt that never really left, the desire to get on top and make it leave once and for all—I had to feed it. I began to take myself more seriously as a performer. I started getting up early, making the rounds. Agents couldn't believe I would camp outside their door before they were in for the day—multiple days in a row.

"You here again, Dominic?" You better believe it, have another picture.

I took acting classes and got involved with St. Mark's Playhouse on Eighth Street, down in the Village. Once, I was working on a scene there from *Death of a Salesman*, and I was reading Biff, and there was this young, fairly handsome actor just up from Omaha who was reading Happy. And he always had his shirt off when we were rehearsing.

"Dominic, this agent keeps asking me to take my shirt off," he said. I told him that the guy probably liked him and it can be that way in the business, and he went back to Omaha.

But I was determined. As serious of a commitment that I took marriage to be, its failing between myself and Camille had helped me to realize where my heart really was. And I tried to convey that seriousness and determination in my work. When a young Bobby Duvall, who we all looked up to and was also performing around the Village then, peeked his head in once to watch a little of a performance I was in, I considered it a high compliment and validating of my dedication. At the time, Bobby was maybe twenty-eight and had been playing the role of a forty-five-year-old senator from the South. It was brilliant.

Another brilliant influence in my life now was the work of Johann Wolfgang von Goethe. I felt I was on the cusp of something, in uncharted territories, and I was seeking all the guidance I could get. I didn't know how to be where I wanted, but I did know it would take persistence. And commitment. Because often in this business, committing to one job could lead to the next. And on committing, Goethe said: "Boldness has power, genius, and magic in it. Begin it now."

And in 1956, what I wanted to begin even more than acting was a singing career.

I started hanging out at a little neighborhood bar on Fordham Road up in the Bronx. I was back to bricklaying and the neighborhood because I had gotten fired from my port job for coming in late after an audition. I didn't really care, and that was not necessarily a good thing. I was still dividing what I considered "real-world responsibilities," such as accountability to an employer, with what I wanted to do in life. Divorce? Shock treatments? Instability? This was not how I had been raised, how people lived where I was from. And the less I enacted of what I was supposed to, the more I saw myself as outside of the traditional "real world." My annulment had shot me out of the gate like a wounded harbinger, and the only bag I had packed was stuffed to the brim with ideas of performing. I had melded all of these strong emotions like hope and love and disappointment and pain into some sort of manifestation poured into pursuit. There was no settling down, no turning back, and no taming this beast.

So I grabbed that microphone, and I went to work. Because when you're on stage with the experts, you need to come up with a purpose. And I think Earl Warren recognized that in me. Earl played with Count Basie and fronted his own quintet down at this little bar in the Bronx, and he let me come up on stage and sing with them. And these guys were sharp. They knew I understood that I wasn't there to try and show off—that I was there to be part of a tight ensemble and learn. It was a fantastic experience, and I could see that I was growing as a singer.

That tiny platform stage in the little saloon down in the Bronx is where I was cutting my teeth. Where I was learning discipline. And these severely underpaid jazz musicians let me keep performing with them. I couldn't say it, but I was extremely grateful and humbled every night.

There was one performance that was a real turning point: Saint Patrick's Day. That particular day, I was introduced on stage by a local comic who gave me flak for what I figured to be my young age and a "perceived lack of experience."

"Here's Dickie Chee-an-ay-see from…" the comic paused and looked at me, "What'd you spend like six weeks on Rikers Island?" He was busting my chops pretty good in front of everyone. But I got up there with that discipline, that form that these accomplished musicians had so graciously let me learn from them. I sang the heck out of "When Irish Eyes Are Smiling" and the place went crazy. Earl Warren's group backed me, and they were swinging hard. That was a great day. And what I realized that day is that under the right conditions, with fantastic musicians, I had the power to win over an audience with a song.

Mac Angelo, who had his own orchestra, came looking for me at my parents' house on Prospect Avenue. Word was traveling that I was paying my dues and he wanted to make me the next Bobby Darin, or maybe even the next Frank Sinatra. So Mac got me a gig singing with him and his orchestra at the Corso Ballroom down on 86th Street. I would go down there on the weekends and let them have it. People were dancing and having a good time while I was up on stage having a ball, feeling like Sinatra.

It felt good to let go and there was a sense of security in this gig I had, performing for these crowds. It was almost as if I had been given a "wall," in the form of a stage, and as long as that wall held, I knew who I was and who they were, and I couldn't get close enough to get attached. There were a lot of people coming down there on the weekends. A lot of girls.

Chapter 3

JEAN

In 1957, if I held the spot just right, I purely existed in the audience. This swinging crowd at the Corso, drenched in chardonnay and chandeliers, the ones who dared the latest of nights to defy early mornings, is where I found my solace. If I could just outlast the weekdays, then I would get at least one more chance to commandeer this continuing voyage of forsaken hurt and responsibility, the journey the passengers and I knew to be real life itself. And sometimes when I was completely surrendered to moment one and nothing more, there was no stage and there was no separation, and I was once again amongst those who couldn't hurt me. It felt good, and that's why I saw her.

I had already put it all together. Jean Vacchio had been down at the Corso and vulnerable for weeks: the makings of a "Frank Sinatra girl" to my "Frank Sinatra." She was

Italian and absolutely beautiful, the kind of girl so stunning that everyone assumes she's alone because the last guy who approached her was knocked off by some foreign prince's henchman. Jean's glass eye was an asset because her sexiness was so confident. Of course, I was the man of the hour, weekends at the Corso, so I had every right to fall head over heels for her—physically speaking.

And that was the thing. The clinging status quo of the '50s still very much inundated my world in New York—so if we were acting on attraction, we were acting in the name of the long haul. At least that's how both of our families saw it. Because in 1957, when you were courting, the ravenous local gossip would swoop in and extrapolate the "facts" before you barely had a chance to introduce yourself. And my family liked Jean. More importantly, my sister liked her.

Frances was raised to only know structure and to attain traditional family order as soon as possible. If this didn't exist, everything was out of order and nothing could make ultimate sense. So when Frances saw her older brother fouling up—because the man was "supposed to take the lead"—not one (Eleanor), but two relationships (a failed marriage with Camille), she had to ensure that the third time was the charm, or her world built on extended family structure would be fouled up too.

She made herself known and I felt it. My family, via Frances's incessant pressuring for "the next step, the next step," bore down on me to do the "right thing"—it wasn't even an either-or situation since we had already been courting for the "committal time period" of a few weeks! I couldn't believe it. Frances had used the premise of Italian tradition to close the loop on me and *force me* into an "arranged marriage." Sheer genius, much to my expense.

But I *had* brought a shame into our family with my unheard-of annulment. And, as the first son of a first son—a coveted placement in Italian families—I did owe it to everyone to set things straight once and for all. Plus, Jean's family really liked me, and they liked my family too—and the whole time I couldn't keep my hands off Jean. Now this wasn't at an R-rated level yet—society in general wouldn't have that—but it was becoming more acceptable to advance things to PG-13, which was good, because seriously, Jean was red hot.

Her constant visceral allure was slickened grease in viscid emotion. In one form or another, it was all rising to a surface I had tried to block out. I was living it up through lust and glamour and shuttered at the pausing realization of love. Making it was job number one, and now I had strung along this Italian beauty in the process. I was a forlorn comet who had entered her orbit: I thought I could break free anytime. But the crushing weight of zeitgeist and family values clenched me in its gravitational pull. All I could do was circle on the fringes. So I looked for escape. I searched for solace once again.

Things were blurred now, the good and the bad. Fear and trepidation fought determination on a daily basis, and a balled-up "all or nothing" spirit emerged. It was fitting then that the role that redirected my life would require everything.

Acting *and* singing. The best of both worlds. A young Hubert Rolling was directing *Guys and Dolls* at Walton High School in the Bronx and he thankfully cast me as Sky Masterson. Thankfully, as in the sense that it was a lead role where I was really allowed to try comedy for the first time. And since comedy makes the heart grow fonder, my heavy heart stood to become outright devoted. And it did, and I was.

Hubert was supplied with no more than a shoestring and masterfully threw the show together within weeks. This was basically community theatre, and we had a nice, full, diverse Bronx crowd. And during the play, I could tell that the audience was really getting into this affordable escapism entertainment.

My character, Sky, has a bet with his buddies in the play that he can take Sister Sarah to Cuba. So at one point, Sister Sarah and Sky are conversing and Sarah asks Sky where he would like to go. And Sky, seeing opportunity knocking, immediately responds with, "How about Havana?" Sarah, completely caught off guard, retorts, "Havana!?" And Sky, defensive at her noticeable deflection in her tone and at the prospect of losing the bet with his buddies, follows with, "Where'd you want to go? Howard Johnson's?" And the audience erupted in applause and laughter.

See, this joke especially hit home for a Bronx audience because everyone knew about the Howard Johnson's on Fordham Road and Southern Boulevard, and they could just picture Sky and Sarah skipping over a tropical getaway and posting up at some diner up the street. And while the Walton High School auditorium was filled with laughter and cheers, I realized a few things. I instantly knew what comedy was about. It's about the truth, about being honest. I actually had not initially realized that the Howard Johnson's line was funny. I just said the line normally, and the comedy took care of itself.

Even bigger, though, I realized my truth. I could look out and see that all types of people in this diverse audience were enjoying the moment, enjoying it together. No matter their race, or religion, or background, everyone, for at least one moment, shared the common bond of a joyful human experience. I could see that theatre was a way to help create these all-important moments; I could see that theatre was necessary. And right then, in the briefest of flashes, I saw past everything inside of me, to the truest soul of my everlasting core, and I knew I was destined to be an actor.

Having observed that I fully applied myself, even in what basically amounted to little-known community theatre, Hubert took me aside afterward and said, "Listen, I'm going to be directing down at the Hilltop Theatre in Maryland this summer—would you like to be an apprentice?" At the time, it was understood, within summer stock hierarchy, that apprentices helped build the sets and possibly—with no guarantee—got an opportunity to fill a walk-on role or two toward the end of the run.

I quickly examined my options. Option one involved not following up on an offer to possibly gain experience and watch the automated Italian tradition factory grind me up and spit me out with a ring on; option two was to spend a summer hauling refrigerators with a shred of a chance at getting to play a role no one would remember. I needed to create some distance from Jean because I just did not want to address that I didn't want to marry her; plus I never really did have anything against refrigerators, so I easily made the decision. And as they say, one job led to another.

And this particular job involved carrying refrigerators. Don Swann was the taskmaster of the production and he liked his refrigerators hauled. Don would say, "You can be on stage someday, but right now, you're going to carry refrigerators!" And I did, all summer. To be fair, though, Don also interwove gum-scraping the theatre seats to break up the monotony. But it was a good experience from an observational stance: I really got a feel for everything that goes into a production and began to appreciate and understand all aspects of theatre that much more.

Plus, I was formulating a plan, as much as I had ever had one. I had initially received an Actors' Equity card through a back door with the merging of the Chorus Equity. Now, if I stuck out two summers of gum and iceboxes, then I would earn the card again, this time for real. I figured I would have really achieved something in my art then; and I often thought of this as I readied my scraper for the freshest of chews.

As illuminating as my departure into the lower rungs of theatre was, everything went dim when I got back to New York. I felt I was changing inside; I actually had this "plan" within my field that I had been working. But that required waiting until the next year's summer stock—which I would have to audition for—before it could be fulfilled. And that meant a year of ducking Jean and our two families breathing a marriage down my neck. Whatever structure I had put together down in Baltimore was in complete disarray now. I just wanted to pursue my art. I wanted to escape. So, I did what many artists who wanted to escape did. I hid out in the Village.

Fortunately for me, the Village was welcoming escapees with open arms. There was a folk music craze going on in the late '50s down there, and it reawakened my singing ambitions. Of course, since I lived only thirteen miles away back in the Bronx, Jean, her reputation—of which *my* structured upbringing would not let me tarnish—and the pressures of settling down so "late in life" were constantly hovering. But at least I was always a subway ride away from a coffee shop haven, a drum circle discussion—an artist's euphoria—so long as you didn't go past a few blocks and step back into the real world, featuring amenities such as "having a job." And as long as I calculatingly spread my time between home and habitat, I could avoid the question that I was ever expected to pop.

All this maneuvering bought me at least a couple months. It was almost as if I were being forced into this artist's lifestyle because I couldn't tell my girlfriend the truth. This is how strong our deep-seated Italian culture was. If I confessed that I didn't want to marry Jean, it would immediately label her with "something wrong"—we had been together off and on for a year. It would also signal to my family that I was a haphazard mess who was just fooling around and not taking my structured upbringing seriously—an unallowable option for a firstborn Italian son who had already annulled a marriage. As the folk craze would tell us, the times were in fact changing, but up in the Italian-laden sections of the Bronx, they hadn't quite yet got the message. So I looked for ways out of New York entirely. If outright avoidance of Jean had worked before, it could work again. But time was running out before I was confronted once and for all with my intentions, and my options were thin.

I scrambled for a singing group audition on Bleecker Street. I must have conveyed all of this pent-up tension I was carrying around through an energetic performance because they instantly hired me and started filling me in on our upcoming tour.

However, I had held out just long enough, and the next day was the audition for the yearly Hilltop summer stock. I went in, bombastic energies channeled, and got hired for that job too. In the midst of all this fight-or-flight, I remembered back to when I had formulated a plan for earning an Equity card. I also knew that apprentices who made it to the second year would definitely have the opportunity to perform major and supporting roles. So, for once in my life, I merely stuck to the plan.

That is, until I met Phyllis Stinchcomb, a Southern belle and fellow apprentice down at the Hilltop. Phyllis was from the South, and she loved my New York accent. We instantly became infatuated with one another's regional nuances, and we liked each other. I even went and met her mother, who was in Baltimore at the time, and we all sat around the piano and fittingly sang "People Will Say We're In Love" from *Oklahoma!* Phyllis's presence awoke me from this stupor of arts-versus-love that I had been drifting through, and while I surely didn't forget about Jean back home, for the time being, I had some form of both.

Now I could earn my Equity card. And I did, doing all kinds of character parts. Hubert directed me in *No Time for Sergeants*; I was in *The Teahouse of the August Moon*; and I played an abusive jazz musician in *Middle of the Night*. I also played the baseball manager in *Damn Yankees*, where I got to incorporate singing too. It was a wonderful time for growth as an actor and I learned that I had a particular penchant for portraying authority figures. Alas, all summers must come to a close, and I headed back to New York, confidence raised and guard lowered.

My first stop on my newfound high was to let Phyllis down gently. After all, I was a *professional* now, having earned my Actors' Equity card, and I wasn't going to have time for little flings—even if they weren't risqué. So Phyllis came up to New York after summer stock and she was very forthright, asking me what my intentions were with her while we sipped coffee in Midtown. We took a walk up Broadway, where *West Side Story* was currently playing, and noticing that stirred me enough to think, "That's where I'm going to be soon anyway!" Still, I was a little saddened to tell Phyllis that Jean was in the picture. Then, Phyllis left and went back to Baltimore. And I suppose I had developed more of an attachment to her then I had realized because when she left, that high that I had rode back to New York on seemed a little lower and my heart seemed just a little heavier.

Nonetheless, I had a job to do. And the next stop on my slightly lowered, but still insurmountable high, my real destination the whole time, was the venerated Actors Studio. For the professional actor—someone, say, like me, now in possession of what I surmised to be the *esteemed* Actors' Equity card—it was the next logical step. Things were lining up. I was putting aside what I thought I didn't need and focusing on what I thought I did. All I had to do was ace the membership audition at the Actors Studio and I would practically be made. Everything would take care of itself, and I would be way too busy for anyone to even start suggesting ideas of marriage again. In this particular plan, I admittingly had not spent as much time with the details.

I decided I would audition with the abusive jazz musician I had portrayed in *Middle of the Night* during summer stock. It was a particularly meaty role amongst my freshly minted repertoire, and it called for a wide range of demonstrated emotion as this jazz musician addressed his wife. There was only one detail that I was not really sure about: the audition itself.

The thing is, I had never liked the audition process. I did not believe in them. I did not believe that you could determine whether someone was right for a role simply by having them "do some lines" on the spot, as opposed to letting them absorb the entire role completely through real performance. I knew there were actors who felt the same way I did, good actors who would not put their "best work" into an audition because the audition process *was* hard work and—as they felt—was undeserving of the talent they would show in a real job. I fervently declared allegiance to this group of acting sandbaggers and unfortunately took a head full of their "wisdom" into the Actors Studio.

Needless to say, I screwed the whole thing up. It was terrible. It was over before it started. I just kept thinking about how much I *had* to get this, how it was make or break—all before I actually went on stage to audition. By the time I got on stage, I was this hybrid acting monstrosity of anger against the audition process, anger against the Actors Studio for holding me to said process, fear of the Actors Studio for believing my career was beholden to them, and simply not knowing where to stand. My only guiding thought was: "You want me to be a member of the Studio? You have to see my work!" Apparently, they did not see my work. And I decided I was never even going to give it a second shot down the line.

And with nowhere to run and nowhere to hide, the responsibilities of an Italian man doing the right thing by his girl and their families came calling. I broke down and told Jean that I did not want to get married. I kept telling her. I even told her right before the wedding. But it was too late. In her mind, her family's mind, and my family's mind—further perpetuated by my sister, no less—we had already committed a long time ago. Jean had even planned out the wedding before it was official. My momentum from summer stock had come to a grinding halt with the Actors Studio exclusion, and I just didn't have it in me to disappoint everyone's ideals.

The wedding was truly incredible. I was playing a groom— the role of a lifetime, so Jean expected. I pleaded with her that it was not going to work, that I just was not ready; but she said, "You've got to do it to save my face." Maybe she thought it would change afterward, that I would change. Maybe she didn't care and just wanted a wedding no matter what. The only thing that I knew for sure was that I had allowed my indecisiveness and unwillingness to confront a brooding issue determine my course for me, and now I was about to commit the biggest farce of my life before two hundred people in a dark Lutheran church because even the Catholics wouldn't have any part of it.

Jean's family gave us the top floor of their house on 119th Street and I moved away after ten days. It was completely ridiculous. I had gone through with a marriage I didn't want, to a really beautiful and trusting girl who I really didn't love, and after a little over a week of just sitting around and not consummating the marriage—because somehow in my expert rationalization, I decided it would have made things worse—I just got up and left. After that, I was sure my family had given up on me. In fact, my sister Frances did, and we didn't speak for a long time. But I didn't care because I was very unhappy—unhappy with my failed relationships, unhappy with my enfeebled trade, unhappy with life in general. So, at twenty-seven years of age, I filed for my second annulment.

Of course, none of this went over too well with Jean. And while some part of her remained steady enough to discern that, yes, it would not work out now, she was fuming. She tried to get even by hiring a lawyer who came up with this cockamamie restitution plan where I would pay Jean fifteen dollars a week for the rest of her life. And since I really had no money anyway and was impractical with it when I did, I said, "Sure, why not?" I couldn't take these kinds of proceedings any longer and was willing to sign whatever to end it. I never saw Jean after that, and she never tried to collect on the deal. And as far as I know, that deal still stands.

The only real embrace I felt I had was from the acting community. I couldn't face my family, though they would have reluctantly accepted me; and after my second annulment, the neighborhood was so small it practically squeezed me out. So I would drop by Hubert Rolling's apartment because surely the embellished truth hadn't traversed all of Manhattan yet, what embellishing possibly still remained, and I needed to keep one foot in the door of the only recent accomplishments I knew. And Hubert showed me this portrait he had of his father or grandfather—I was too emotionally tangled to pay attention which one—and said, "My father was married five or six times." I exhaled, knowing that there were men obviously way "more confused" than I could ever be; but I also noticed that this idea of multiple marriages had given me relief.

I sought inspiration. I would go down to lower Manhattan where the "Olde New York" buildings still were and would think of Hawthorne and Emerson and the Revolutionary War. The fighting spirit. The idea of creating something new from the ashes. I would sit on the steps of the U.S. Customs House and sense the progress of history all around me, the irreversible inertia of a destined path. There was a horizon, and admitting this was enough for right now. I knew I couldn't let this serene part of me go, so I applied for a job that would keep me in the area. Fortuitously, I landed a check-pressing position with Hanover Trust Bank—the fortuitous aspect being that I landed this position alongside another young actor named George C. Scott.

It was a struggling actor's job, and George was a leader amongst us struggling actors. He was working in the Off-Broadway show *Children of Darkness* and had just had his first child. I got to know him through playing poker at his house and could quickly see that he was a wonderful human being—and dedicated. He got results. George was the guy who spoke up.

One of the night supervisors had been hassling us actors at the bank, denying us cigarette breaks or something—it was a "thing" for hip actors to smoke Gauloises cigarettes at the time. Being struggling actors, some of us were already on edge and needed those breaks. So George went over to the supervisor and said, "You know, you really should help these guys out. And if you don't, I'm going to punch you right in the nose." And the guy got scared of George and caved. We couldn't believe it: a struggling actor who had stood up for what little he visibly had! It was no wonder that George soon thereafter landed a role in *Comes a Day* with Judith Anderson on Broadway, that his performance was received with glowing reviews. The man had courage and resoluteness and brought it to all of his work. The next thing we knew, he was in Hollywood. I had initially wanted to stay in Lower Manhattan because I had found it inspiring. I ended up learning to be confident and fearless in my own work from my friend George C. Scott.

It was 1959 and times were in fact changing. It was a little more acceptable to be promiscuous, as long as it wasn't too blatant or anything. I took this first crack in the wall of traditional sexual mores as a license to thrill. I had seen two marriages quickly crumble into shambles and had decided that was it. My adherence to my structured upbringing had gotten me nothing but misery, plus I was carving out my new identity in the free-spirited arts now anyway, so I met Helen through a friend of a friend's wife, we hung out, and we moved in together. And then Helen was pregnant. Then she told me she wanted an abortion.

While the scrutinizing of sexual conduct was beginning to lighten up some, the practice of abortion was very controversial and still highly illegal. Because this was New York City, however, there were always "places" you could go if you knew about them—but I did not want her to do it. Even the mere mention of an abortion sent me into a sheer panic. It was one thing for me to bend on Italian traditions and move in with Helen, but it was far, far another to, in my eyes, disrupt what would be my natural lineage.

I begged her to consider having the baby. I even went to my parents and confessed everything, expecting they would somehow step in and reprimand Helen into keeping the baby, bailing me out like they had before. Interestingly enough, they did not seem too upset. They seemed to understand that I had done what I had because I truly was not ready for another marriage—perhaps word of the changing times had finally started to trickle into the old neighborhood. But that was where the extent of their sympathy stopped. To them I was a man, two marriages failed to show, and I was to handle it on my own. So after a very deliberate and sober rumination, I respected Helen's decision and took her to one of those "places."

Pure agony. That was all I felt while I sat in the waiting room at that Bronx house. I just stared at the wallpaper and kept saying, "This is wrong, this is wrong." I knew Helen was in the next room taking chances with her health. Not only was it an illegal procedure, but back then they didn't have what they have now, so it could be very dangerous. That's why I tortured myself and forced myself to stay, to make sure she was all right.

And because it was so unknown, I had, without a doubt, resolved that my child was being taken away from me. All I thought I knew was that I was a father, and I was being stripped of my family. In the midst of my anguished persecution, I remember picturing fathers who did the right thing and raised their children—how I envied them, and how I wouldn't be one. I also had a thought that maybe Helen knew that I wasn't ready to be one either. This notion, though, was quickly enveloped and overridden with guilt and resentment that I was helpless because *my* decision and my feelings didn't count since I didn't get my way. It was very dark, very confusing, and very upsetting up in that Bronx house that night, and when Helen came out of the room and said she was okay, I took her home and never saw her again.

I never saw part of myself again either. Part of my structured upbringing was now tainted, and I would never get that back. By relenting to what was becoming acceptable, I had given away what I knew to be true. I couldn't keep a marriage intact, I couldn't hold an acting career steady, and now I couldn't even shack up right—like so many of the people around me did effortlessly. Sure, I had seen *some* achievement—even the guys back in the neighborhood who would shoot dice and run from the cops got away sometimes—but maybe I really had been on the wrong path. Maybe there really was something to this "security and sensibility first" that I had been hearing about my whole life.

But what was there before all of this? Could I even see past this pain that dwelt, that had found its home? What I believed in, what I thought I believed in, what I took and acted upon—it just wasn't working. The problem had to be with me. If I was supposed to be who I thought, surely

I would be that by now, at least always stepping across the pebbles of success and not falling headfirst into the raging current of failure that had grown accustomed to my momentary unsure perch. In my traumatically tinted scope, life had become even and, given the chance, would not hesitate to pass me by. Why had I deviated from who I was supposed to be, whom I was *originally* supposed to be? This was a new decade: enough dreaming, I had to get serious. This time, I would follow the plan, the real plan, the plan that had been laid before me since the beginning: I would go to school to become a schoolteacher.

There was something to it. There was absolutely something to structure, formality, security. I could see why loving hands had wanted to guide me here the whole time. I knew what the next day would bring. And while I was now pursuing a degree in education through night school at Brooklyn College, I even allowed myself to breathe, sanctuary existing once more. There were always four walls and a roof, and my failures and pitiful triumphs would not find me in here. But my real self would. So as I settled in, I would thumb through the course catalog and accumulate the education regiment with increasing servitude while eyeing the drama program's offerings with progressive wholeheartedness. I did not fight this inclination and eventually I awoke: "My God, I started acting in the '50s—why don't I maybe go back into acting?"

I could discern that the incisiveness of looming rejection was hindering my ability. I knew I could sing, but after blunting my momentum and botching the Actors Studio audition, I wanted to find out what exactly had me made me so nervous on that decisive day and where my authentic talent hid. Doctor Bernard Barrow's Introduction to Theatre course felt right at home since I wore disillusionment well. Bernie, as we would call him, also played Mr. Ryan on *Ryan's Hope* and spoke lovingly about the theatre. He would fill the classroom with visions and tales of the stage, and I would imagine myself being cast in his stories' major roles. Bernie became a friend in the theatre world when I needed one, and he reinvigorated my desire for acting prowess.

I continued serving out my education degree, now slowly and blindly stumbling my way heart-forward into the theatre world again. And with no attempt at deviation through desired companionship—Jean too fresh in mind even if I could fully swallow my self-induced situational poison with Helen—I regained focus, and the traumatically tinted lenses started to lighten. Then, I joined the theatre group at Brooklyn College and met one of the most influential mentors in my life: Professor Wilson Lehr.

Wilson Lehr taught me about what an actor should understand *once* a commitment was made to theatre. He taught me about preparation, about the complete focus an actor must have when preparing a role. Wilson was a man of education and a man of the arts: he was a writer and a director and had performed in television when shows were broadcast live. He taught drama in the English department, but what he conveyed was ability, success, and belief in one's self. And just as I was clasping at the remnants of hope and needed it most, he believed in me too.

Both Wilson and Bernie were always taking me aside and giving me practical tips—I was extremely fortunate to have such caring and interested mentors in my life. Incrementally, I surrendered my stealth emotions, compensating this established void by flocking to the comforts of my acting past. On my previous comedic successes with an audience, I would ask: "How do I know if it's going to be funny?" And Wilson would reply, "The audience will tell you." And he was right. He knew.

Wilson also knew that I was limited by my lack of confidence. He taught me how to have a confident walk, how to have a leading man's walk, how to be proud of myself physically and display it—how to commit excellently to every gesture, to all that I did. He said, "When your hand goes out, go all the way out." He sat down with me between classes and went over "to be or not to be" from *Hamlet*. He taught me that the speech had to be from the gut. Wilson had me play Garcin in Sartre's *No Exit* even when I was too young to know what I was doing; he said it was what I had to do. He challenged me to stretch my acting muscles, and I slowly put away my old acting self and started to become an actor reformed. Wilson took all the Bronx out of me and made me stage-worthy. He taught me to be proud; he made me feel good.

Since I was older than most of the other students, Wilson thought I could play the supporting and commanding role of Colonel Vershinin from Chekhov's *Three Sisters*. Wilson explained, "Dominic, you've got to have flair to play this part. Vershinin's a military man and he thinks he's important. He's very, very Russian, and he comes in and charms the sisters and he just takes over the place." Brooklyn College was even bringing in a guest director from Wales for the production: Philip Burton, Richard Burton's stepfather. All of the school's best actors were in the play, including a young Herb Edelman, and it was a big deal for the school. I was very excited to be playing the romantic hero Vershinin—a type of part I didn't often get the chance to do—and I was ready to bring it.

In the third act, I had a *very heavy* scene with Masha, who was played by Deborah Gordon, a terrific actress. The scene was about my going away. It was really intense, but I felt I was up for it. One night, Philip Burton dropped by the dressing room before the show and said, "Dominic, you're doing it beautifully, wonderfully. Nice job. But the third act—you've got to think about it. You've got to show more emotion. It's just not..." and then he broke off. Switching tones, he said, "Why do you want to be an actor? Maybe you shouldn't be an actor."

I wondered how visible all of the blood rushing to my head was to him. I mustered some of my greatest acting ability up until then and calmly, for what passed as calm at the time, told him, "I'll try it again tonight, Mr. Burton." Meanwhile a scorched earth of challenged livid resentment rose inside. In my opinion, I was one of the top actors in the school and he was lucky to have me! How could he tell me that!? So I bottled up whatever I could reign in of my personal inferno and made a note to pop the cap in what would now be tonight's especially effervescent, audience-stunning third act.

And after the show, Philip breezed by the dressing room again and said, "Ehh, that's a little better. Maybe you should take some acting lessons or something." Curiously, this slight, this acting abjection, while still finding me sensitive and tender to the critic's eye, did not have the same effect as once before. I merely accepted the comment, knowing who I was as an actor, and moved on. By beginning to relinquish ego, I was gaining something much more: humility.

While this was an important first step, the lesson was not yet fully learned. The education curriculum had run its course and I was set to graduate in 1961. Just before I did, however, Wilson Lehr offered me a role in the Adult Education Theatre Association. We would be traveling to Greenland to perform at army and navy bases, and it really was an honor I hadn't expected. Excited at this surprising opportunity, I immediately told him I'd do it.

I had done a scene from *The Visit* with Bernie at Brooklyn College in which I played a priest. When the church bell rang I just went haywire, knocking over the altar in the process. And Bernie stated, "You've got to learn how to contain that." It was true because I still had a tendency to act on impulse, on the cusp of current emotion. And not just in theatre, but in life in general too. I was headed to Greenland, had been talking to "Miss Beatnik 1959," who just happened to be in one of my classes, and was playing the lead in *The Male Animal*—which was appropriate, because I had not even begun to unleash what had been building inside.

Chapter 4

MERLE

"Are you sure you want to do this?"

It was so easy to just up and commit with a Greenland-bound traveling production. Didn't know much about the place, and really, I didn't need to. Wilson Lehr's question was more directed toward something I did "know" a little more about: marriage.

As fate would have it, I was not the only would-be artist whose homely structured existence had driven them into refugee-status down in the Village. In fact, our very own Miss Beatnik 1959—as awarded by the *Village Voice*—had been amongst us for years now. And fate, not content to rear head, see shadow, and run, had further intervened by having Miss Beatnik 1959 and me take Improvisation at Brooklyn College simultaneously.

She called herself "Angel" and I had to get closer. I knew you didn't just earn a Miss Beatnik title from answering the right question—you had to be around, and she was. I followed her into coffee shops, this razor-sharp exotic brunette, and her conversations would blow my mind. She was sensuous, the hippest, *and* had a genius IQ: no wonder I was confronted by other guys because of her. "Don't bother with them, they're dangerous," she would say. And she was tough. It's funny how the constant presence of a nineteen-year-old, pot-smoking, unabashedly daring, artistic epitome of *the* modern woman can make you want to forget your troubles. Merle Molofsky had it all—of course I wanted to do this.

And she did too. When we went to get the marriage license, the carefree sentiments of the 1960s Village not having filled out the full corners of the city just yet, the man at the desk said to her, "You realize that this man has been married twice before?" And she quickly returned, "Yeah, but I don't care." Pure embodied rambunctiousness, and I loved it.

Merle was a beautiful bride. We got married right in her parents' house. Merle's grandparents lived on the ground floor, but they wouldn't attend. Orthodox Jews were not too crazy about mixed marriages. Merle's parents—while Jewish—attended, however. Her father, Sam, was a kind older man who worked in a bookstore. Her mother, Sima, on the other hand, was hard. Sima had lost some relatives in Poland during the Holocaust, and it was to my understanding that this had been deeply affecting. Though Sam and Sima were very leftist and secular, and Sima notably anti-religious, they both got along great with my own parents—who themselves did not attend either, two weddings having been enough.

Still, it was perfect and beautiful, and there was enough happiness for me to subside. And when I got back from Greenland, I was on a roll. I had *the* girl from the Village waiting for me, and I graduated from Brooklyn College with the most promising future ahead that had ever lain before. I went straight over to HB Studio, an advanced actors workshop and study, and enrolled. They wanted me to start at the beginning of the curriculum, with the intro stuff like "smelling the coffee cup," but I told them forget it: I had ten-plus years acting experience under my belt and I wanted to go right into scene study. Then, the brilliant acting instructor Walt Witcover stepped in and got it approved—and forced me to confront myself once and for all.

Walt had me play a killer in *Climate of Eden.* It was a scene disguised to be romantic, but really my character was supposed to kill the woman in the end. So, I thought I would unite all untapped rage, and when it came time, I shouted at the top of my lungs. The actress got so genuinely scared that she started backing away and knocking things over: it was chaos. And after we finished, her now truly upset, Walt gave his customary scene critique before the whole class and said, "Dominic, I didn't believe a word you said."

And nobody in the class said anything—for about three or four days. It was just too incredible. Everyone had just witnessed this unbridled ferocity, this real act of terror that had caused sheer panic in a scene partner, only to have it dismissed by the instructor as basically "pathetic." Whoever made the next move was almost admitting this quality about themselves.

At home, I thought: "What does he mean, 'didn't believe a word'? I've been on stage; I've evoked audience response—I've made people laugh!" Then, after pondering this for a while, I thought back to when Philip Burton at Brooklyn College had told me that I had to show more emotion. But did I not scare the actress in my scene? Did she, perhaps, not think that there was an uncontrollable element put forth that might have a tinge of such a heinous act? Maybe there was something I was holding back that I had never addressed when performing comedies; maybe I did have something to learn when it came to performing drama.

So the next time in class when it was my time to work, Walt paused and said to me, "Dominic, there's somebody in your family that you were close to." And Grandpa Domenico had only passed a few years before, and I was very close to Grandpa, so I told him about that. And Walt said, "Tell me about your grandfather. What do you remember about him? Describe him." And I started to describe my grandfather and how he was strong with his hands, with his hammer and chisel. All of these memories suddenly flooded me. And Walt could see that he was getting somewhere so he said, "*Tell* me about his hands. *Tell* me about your grandfather." And as I began to recount the precious memories and saw the unattainable innocence that singed their fading boundaries, the tears began to flow. All of my confused and tangled emotions came out, and I just sat and cried for three or four minutes. The class was kind of stunned; there was silence, no one said anything. And Walt observed all of this and said, not just to me, but the whole class, "You see that? That's what I want. That's what you have to get."

We did a scene from Seán O'Casey's *Shadow of a Gunman* where I played the Irish poet Donal Davoren, who is writing a poem while a young girl tries to flirt with him. And Walt stopped us in the middle of the scene and said, "What are you doing, Dominic? What are you doing right now?" And I told him I was writing a poem. "Then write it," he said. "Really write the poem." And that's when I learned how to play the moment.

In a following class, I was doing a scene from *La Ronde* with Mies Walevejn. At one point, she beckoned me to bed and I almost jumped over the table. I had learned how to play the moment freely. And in that particular moment, I wanted to jump over furniture and hop in the sack!

So, I had a lot of emotion, but I had to learn how to control it. And this was the beginning. I was learning how to act and trust the moment. And I wasn't the only one either. Two of my lifelong friends were learning alongside me at HB Studio: Dimo Condos and Steve Zimbler.

If I ever needed a special item for wardrobe or just something quick to keep warm, Dimo was the guy. As a fellow aspiring actor, Dimo kept a closet full of clothes over on Bank Street and I would just shoot over to his place if I was ever in a pinch. To me, this was such an act of kindness, to just freely lend anything I needed—this being amongst the somewhat questionable brood of struggling New York actors—so it was with great reluctance, and ultimately resigned acceptance, that I returned the favor to Dimo and helped him get into the Actors Studio.

Having faced my own trial by fire with my previous Actors Studio audition, and having been around enough to know that the Actors Studio pretty much survived on the red meat of relentless criticism, Dimo had made a request that was the equivalent of me throwing him to the sharks. But he wanted it, very much, so I worked on a scene with him from *J.B.* by Archibald MacLeish, and when we went to go perform for the audition, going up those steps filled with teaching gurus from the Studio was like passing through a gauntlet. And two things happened that day: Dimo was accepted; and, because Dimo was a sensitive actor, it destroyed his career.

Whereas Dimo approached his acting with a more intensive perspective, my friend Steve seemed to enjoy the lighter side of entertainment, and naturally we would get caught up in humorous and whimsical endeavors. We once were rehearsing a scene from *Becket*, the play that Richard Burton and Peter O'Toole had done together on film. We were at Steve's apartment, and he had this enormous poodle that could sprawl out the length of the couch, and I was wearing a blanket, pretending I was cloaked and riding horseback, and there was a knock at the door.

"Oh!" Steve said, "I forgot I had to show these people the room today because I'm moving out." So Steve opens the door and in walk these two tough-looking Brooklynese guys and their green-dressed, gangster-affiliated-looking girl accomplice and they say, "We wanna see da ting." So Steve takes the two guys in the back and the girl in the green dress sits on the couch, crosses her legs, and chews her gum.

These Brooklynese guys must have been all right with leaving "their girl" in the other room because they seemed to do this quick observation of: two guys, alone and playing dress-up, and a monstrous poodle on the couch...you never know. So they left and it was just me and this girl, and her smacking gum and staring above my head. And where her "train of thought" had visually landed was on Steve's print of the famous Van Gogh sunflower painting hanging on the wall. Now this might have been *the* de facto piece of home décor at the time. Everyone had it. You could literally step outside of most places and buy it on the street for forty cents. And she just smacked the gum into oblivion, finally putting it all together, and said, "Who paints?"

I couldn't believe it. I tried not to crack up. I think I was able to coherently sputter, "Oh, it's something we just tossed off." And the guys came in off the terrace and they all left, and Steve and I laughed for half an hour. "Who paints?" It was classic.

Steve and I would hang out at White Castle and celebrate little milestones like how broke we were, and being able to have some humility about the whole thing and not lose sight of day-to-day joys helped to keep us going. Steve was also more business-oriented than both Dimo and me and had seen what had happened with Dimo. Knowing that he too was impressionable by overt criticism, Steve began to go in a more business-minded direction, drifting toward stocks and management.

Between Walt Witcover's eye-opening revelations on my acting and the support and friendship of my two acting peers, I was thankfully afforded the opportunity to freely grow as an actor, and as a person. This freeing opportunity of growth was also partly enabled by the fact that Merle had been home much of this time, pregnant with our first child.

Rebecca Chianese was born at Brooklyn Jewish Hospital in July 1962. It was such a wonderful day; I was so proud—to see this child, this daughter of mine, to finally know those tears of joy. As I quickly realized, though, marriage was a partnership, and Merle and I also had our first culture clash on this day as well.

There was a slight altercation over naming Rebecca. It was very much a part of the Christian culture my heritage was based in to name a child after a living relative—the name Dominic, for instance, had been passed down before. However, in Merle's stricter Jewish orthodoxy, naming a child after a living relative was almost superstitious. On this point, Merle was firm.

I had told myself I was going to respect her traditions, as I might encounter them as we go, so we named our daughter Rebecca after Merle's aunt who was no longer with us. I was so overcome with happiness that I didn't really stop too long to dwell on this naming acquiescence, but I did pause just long enough to notice that this was the first time I had seen Merle really take an unrelenting stance on anything and it reminded me a little of her mother, who drew a hard line. Still, it was such a momentous and blessed occasion, and we all celebrated because now we were a family—which meant I was finally a family man, which meant it was time to get to work.

As a husband, and now a father, I realized that I had to support my family and acting wasn't paying me anything. I thought I had found a way to please everyone: I had earned my bachelor's degree in education, Merle wanted security for our new daughter and herself while she took care of her, and my father had always wanted me to be a schoolteacher, so I applied to the New York City school system and was immediately hired. In this new role of breadwinner, everyone would win—except for me and my dream of acting.

But nevertheless, I had seen this role before: the countless men in my family who had come before me, those who had sacrificed what they wanted for the good of their families—it was almost more sweet than bittersweet to step into my designated birthright, to assume what had been proven and was waiting all along. I had been adamant in the beginning with Merle and her parents that I wanted to pursue acting, that the road might be long and sparse, so it was no surprise that their acceptance of my shift seemed to come more amenably than my own.

I had been out of the public school system picture for a while, so all I had were my ideals. I went in thinking that teaching would be the equivalent of a little red schoolhouse where you had complete authority. Leave it to the 1960s New York City public school system to completely shatter any quaint and manageable notion of learning with an extreme and personal prejudice.

They assigned me what were considered the supposedly slowest kids: a fifth-grade class down in a dicey section of Brooklyn. These children were not up to the grade reading level of their peers. They were all Hispanic and African American, except for Asher, who was an immigrant from Israel and was clearly bright. They were not completely slow as they had all been written off to be; there were understanding children amongst them. But this was easily and often eclipsed by the facts that they were undernourished, underprivileged, and often came in hungry—and all of this broke my heart.

I tried to reach them to no avail. I would come home to Merle with this genuine concern that I just wasn't making a difference. I would explain to her how I even tried to use drama—something I knew—to sublimate the studies, but the school would only allow for so much detour from the approved and scheduled curriculum. Merle, however, knew no such bounds. She was a modern woman after all. This was Miss Beatnik 1959 I had in this apartment, and she welcomed the opportunity to subvert the system from the comforts of her living room.

"Why don't we take the play that we had at Brooklyn College—*The Caucasian Chalk Circle*," Merle exclaimed. Now this was a fairly political play, mind you, and these were fifth-grade students who were still struggling with fifth-grade texts. But none of this mattered to Merle. She simply replied to all of this, "We'll take out all the political stuff and I'll rewrite it for you." And she did. And it worked.

These fifth graders' eyes were glowing with ambition when I told them to put away the readers because we were going to do "scripts." Something had gotten through. Perhaps it was the break in the ceaseless monotony of prepared and expected "learning" that in some way ignited hope for something new.

Everybody in the class got a part. They got into it; they would ask, "How do you say this word?" and "How do you say that word?" I had inadvertently just assigned the world's most interesting vocabulary lesson, apparently. It was a process, and of course, this being the rougher part of Brooklyn, not everything was suddenly picturesque—I still had the hard-head to deal with.

There was this one boy who had kept silent the entire year: he said nothing in class and was expected to be moved forward with the rest of the "delinquents" when the grade level was "complete." But even something arose in him when he saw everyone getting into the play, albeit his reaction was negative. One day, during one of our rehearsals, and out of nowhere, he cursed me out. Admittedly, I still had some of the street in me, mine hailing from the Bronx, and I immediately felt I had to save face before the other children in order to lose no ground I had gained. I also thought I might have fun with this minor outburst and mix in some theatricalities.

I reached for my ruler, which the children understood meant desk-smacking time—because it had previously proven as the last resort, and often only means, for getting these children to pay attention. However, this time there was no smack, and instead I overly pretended like I was going to "get him"—much in the farce-nature of the tempted cook who wields a rolling pin—and proceeded to let him lead our chase around the classroom. The entire class was laughing and clapping and the boy ran out of the room.

But he didn't come back either. And being newish, and still working through relinquishing some of my old ideals on teaching and the school system, I assumed there was some sort of set procedure for this—that the boy had merely gone on to wander the halls for the remainder of the day until he had been absorbed back into the standard education process somewhere else. After two days of not showing back up, however, I looked into it and found out from Principal Pincus that they had transferred the boy out of my class.

And the principal confronted me on what I had done, and I told him that I considered it a breakthrough that the boy even had any sort of reaction at all, even if it was profane. Principal Pincus did not want to hear it. There was one way of doing things, and as a teacher, mine was not an option. I was a little humbled by this experience, that I couldn't just dash headfirst into the winds of education and expect to chart my own flight, and I somewhat considered this as I returned to my classroom with the rest of the students and resumed our clandestine production.

When the time came to perform *The Caucasian Chalk Circle*, I invited the rest of the school down to the auditorium—them not sure what to expect, rogue fifth-grade casts performing college-level plays not the first thing to register in their minds. And those students came through. Not just for me, but for each other. I only had to step on stage once, before the show, to assure Jose, the student playing the sergeant, that he could do it. And the curtain went up, and he did.

Asher played the judge and if anybody missed a line he was right on it, giving them their cue. These children had actually worked hard at something, something school-related, and nobody had ever believed they were capable of something like this. At the end of it, people were crying. I was crying. There were standing ovations for these children. They had put the whole show together. Other teachers, who probably understood the defiant implications of what they had just seen, stood up. In this moment, in their acceptance and moving victory amongst peer and superior, these impossible and forgotten students, the ones cast aside who had been counted out, stood proudly with each other and believed in themselves. They were on top of the world.

A couple days later I got a request to see Principal Pincus in his office. Mr. Pincus made it clear: "Dominic, you can't do plays with them anymore." Never mind the tremendous ovation or boosted morale, creative arts were not on the agenda at the time. So I stuck around for a few more weeks, then tendered my resignation. It was too sad to watch these students, along with all the others, fit back into the mold of predetermined education. They had been covertly granted permission to step out of the fold and breathe the fresh air of open possibility, and I had gone with them. I just couldn't watch that be undone. I wasn't cut out to follow their rules as a teacher, and I knew that any prolonging of the truth was a disservice to the students and to myself. I knew, deep down, that I wasn't following my heart.

So I followed it—right into summer stock. I had gotten into a play called *Moby Dick—Rehearsed* at the Robin Hood Theatre in Arden, Delaware, and was instantly and temporarily transformed to about as far away from a schoolteacher as you can get. My character, Queequeg, was a scurvy ol' sea lad: head shaved and covered in tattoos. I felt I was getting a chance to ventilate some of the suppressed, buttoned-down adherence—whatever amount it was I actually adhered to—from my previous profession. I could breathe that fresh air of openness and possibility that my students and I had briefly enjoyed together. It was fun to play the savage.

What I didn't realize when I started was: that's where the fun only began. Because this was a summer stock production, budgets were always of immediate concern, the shoestring ensued, and accordingly, we had actors doubling up and switching turns at narrating throughout. Needless to say, this can be slightly overwhelming for the lesser-experienced working actor and can connote and heighten the ever-present element of uncertainty during the show. Needless to say, this happened.

Toward the end of the show when the whale was sighted, Jack Ryland, who had been narrating and playing the character of Ishmael, had to be present in the boat. Thus, Harold Cherry, another actor in the play who would get nervous in rehearsals and recite his lines in front of a mirror, was supposed to step in for narration duty at this point. And Herb Voland, who played Captain Ahab, yelled, "Thar she is!" And we all jumped in the boat. Then you could hear the sound effects of the thunder and waves crashing, the storm howling; the tension was mounting: the audience was silent—they were really into this scene.

And this was Harold's cue for the line, "Midnight, the foc'scle watch..." And we're all waiting in the boat for it, and Harold stumbles out with, "Midnight, the foc...the foc...the foc...the foc..." He said it four times; he couldn't say the word "foc'scle." I practically dug my nails in the set to keep from laughing. Herb, as Ahab perched in the mast, broke character and just slid down the pole. We were supposed to perform a song about the whale, but everyone was laughing so hard they couldn't sing. Finally, Harold belted out, "...the foc'scle watch." But by then the play was pretty much ruined. And the director was irate; he went screaming out of the theatre. It was good to be back.

Merle, on the heels of undermining the educational system with her rewritten play—and us living fairly comfortably from my lingering teacher's pay—encouraged me that *now* was the time to pursue the arts. She could see that I had returned from summer stock galvanized, and knew how the process of securing an acting job *could* be—my lingering teacher's pay only lasting so long. So, we decided to dabble in the art world together and went to see the play *Desire Under the Elm,* starring Colleen Dewhurst and a fresh-from-Hollywood George C. Scott.

I never considered myself an aggressive person. I would usually just let things come as they may, and if they didn't, I wouldn't. Merle, however, was not this way. She insisted I go talk to George about getting a job, that I take advantage of a professional relationship now that he was a known actor. But I just couldn't bring myself to do it. I couldn't picture skulking in, me, the one between the two of us who was still working on the "outside," now groveling for a chance to prove that I was, at minimum, capable of sufficing on an acceptable professional level. I was infringing on a friend. That's how I saw it. But, as usual, Merle had a different idea. She consistently told me I should see him. She wouldn't have it otherwise. She drew that hard line.

So I went back to see the show by myself. And afterward, Merle's voice still ringing in my ears and my knowing what lie in wait back home if I didn't follow through, I went backstage and knocked on the dressing room door. And Colleen Dewhurst opened it, took one look, and said, "What do you want?" I was already on the defensive—not good. I meagerly offered up, "I'd like to see George." She turned and faced back into the dressing room, "George, somebody's here to see you." I had been forced into the moment of truth. It had arrived.

He recognized me right away: "Good to see you. How are you, Dominic? What can I do for you?"

I humbly asked, "Well…can I give you my picture?"

"Of course, give me your picture!" George proclaimed. "No question about it. We'll look at it. We'll find something." George was also a current star on the hit television show *East Side/West Side*, which was shot here in New York. Three weeks later, I was on it too.

It was 1963 and my first on-camera job, and I was playing a no-good boyfriend to Louise Troy's character—herself, another star of the somewhat controversial show. I was supposed to visit Louise's character at her apartment— showing up in my deadbeat manner with a paltry bag of groceries, knocking on the door, and facing George C. Scott's character, who would ward me off with a look of: "You shouldn't be with this woman." It was a small role but pivotal to the storyline—the teleplay dealt with a lot of socially charged issues—made all the more difficult by having to convey what I was supposed to without using words.

Nonspeaking parts on television: this was all new territory for me. And after the first take, the director said, "Let's try it one more time, Dominic." Trying it "once more" meant I'd better get it right. And it was make-or-break time, so I looked around the set and thought, "Maybe I'll pretend it's a play— that I'm in a play going down the hall in a tenement house." I'd been in tenements and could relate, so I went with what I knew. And on the second take, I opened the door and walked right in, and I could tell by the look on George's face that I nailed it. He gave me a look like, "Okay, kid, you're all right."

George had gone out on a limb for me; he was putting part of his reputation on the line by vouching for me, and I felt good that I could repay him by coming through with the performance they needed. I felt good that I had done a good job. And after the scene finished shooting and the exhilaration of my first and successful TV run wore down, George and I talked briefly in the dressing room. "We've got to do it again sometime," George cheered. But we never did. And just because we never worked together again didn't change what I already knew: he was a real friend.

Now, I had a decision to make. Merle was about to have our second child, and my first priority was her and our children. But I just couldn't fathom dooming myself once more to the powerlessness of public school teaching—no matter what kind of security it offered our family. I felt I had honestly prepared Merle, and to a lesser degree, her family, for the potential stretches of hardships that ensued when I announced, in the beginning, that I was going to be an actor. And Merle had been supportive at first; but with our family about to increase in size and her unexpected and fast resolve from carefree Village actor to home life, this created tension. If she forsook her dream for the good of our family, she felt it was the right thing for me to do too.

I needed something to show for my ability to expediently move to the next gig, that my art could at least get us by. Another child was incoming and I had to have something

lined up or I would be out of excuses for avoiding the trappings of a normal job. The work aspect had never bothered
me; but after the teaching experience I had gone through, I
knew how soul crushing and career debilitating a nine-to-five
could be to the aspirant artist. Time was short. The pressures
were mounting fast. Merle was demanding security, and I had
nothing on the horizon except the uncharted and unwav-
ering responsibilities of a growing family.

The Village offered refuge once more. I ducked into
Gerde's Folk City over on Bleecker Street, where the world
couldn't follow me in and had to wait at the door. Merle and I
had often been there—back when I would chase Miss Beatnik
around the Village, when unburdened passion nourished
us anew. Seeing new fresh-faced artists get up and perform,
not knowing what lay ahead for them except song and verse,
rekindled the dimming light of my artistic identity. I got a
guitar; I got up the courage to perform at the open mic; I
reached to my roots and sang an Italian song. And afterward,
the owner, Mike Porco, came over and said, "I never heard of
an Italian folk singer!" I told him I was really just an actor in
the wings, and he offered me a job.

Our son was born in 1964, and Merle and I immediately
went into our usual naming dilemma. This time, I felt I had
the upper hand, having let Merle take the lead with Rebecca,
so I said, "Listen, I gotta name him Dominic." And in this
particular instance I must have pleaded my case just right,
because I was able to finagle a compromise. We named him
Dominic, but Merle insisted that we would call him "Dovy."

I had successfully passed down a family name unto my beautiful new son, and I had managed to secure a position as a part-time emcee in a respected folk venue. Life was okay, I unconvincingly thought.

Now or never. That's what I told myself when I went to audition for *Oliver!* on Broadway. The role of Sowerberry the undertaker had opened up, and I gave it everything. I channeled all of my angst, all of my hope, and all of my experience—and I slowly moved up the ranks. It came down to just me and one other actor. And after this extensive audition process, the stage manager approached me and said, "Dominic, I want to talk you." We went out into the hall and he said, "Dominic, I know you can do this, but we have to go with the other guy."

The funny thing about rejection is how you are never really prepared for it, but when it happens it can feel so availably familiar that sometimes you handle it with the comfort of an old pro. I didn't really have much of a telling reaction to the stage manager's news: I just sort of accepted it as a decision and left. And when I stepped out onto the sidewalk, right there on the corner of 44th Street, I took a look at the sweeping world, realized I would never make it as an actor supporting his family, and sat down on the curb and cried.

I never thought about budgets. I actually hated the word "budget," the particular heaviness of its real-world grounding that would forever limit my unrestricted soar. I wouldn't even bother with unemployment collection—which I was entitled to from time to time due to my various acting runs—because

I could not bring myself to sit still, fill out all the forms, and wait around to be processed in some low-level lighting vacuum—otherwise known as a local government office. There was something else that I seemed to be relinquishing when handing in those completed documents of unread legal jargon, something so pertinent to my cause that when I would potentially and finally receive these coveted get-out-of-work-free checks—as self-labeled from observance of the family bricklaying work ethic, albeit the same family who would encourage me to collect said checks when my family needed it, and of whom I ultimately didn't believe *really* meant it—the trade-off didn't seem half-fair. I'd rather starve.

Conflicted, I scrapped together some endless middle road out of sheer desperation. I still had my Folk City gig periodically, and I decided that I would have to give teaching another try—this time in a substitute role. To me, this was succeeding as a father. I was technically making ends meet and hadn't fully vanquished my dream just yet, more like tempered it off into a temporary holding pattern. And with just a little more of a convincing argument this time, I thought life was okay.

However, Merle had not been quite so convinced. My brief inroads with *East Side/West Side* and television "stardom" had come and gone, and Merle was now watching her husband not utilize his college degree to fully support his family comfortably by pursuing a permanent teaching position.

A rift opened. Merle was only twenty-four and had just gone from dancing down the primrose path of the Green-wich artistic sanctuary to a full-time stay-at-home mother of two. Everything for her was new and unpredictable. She would see me leave every day, come home, and hope that I had done enough for us to get by without worrying. My plan was more "get by," keep a slowly burning candle lit for my dream of somehow, some way overcoming the stacking odds and making it—right now in the form of Folk City—and maybe have to "worry" in the interim.

There were blowups. Like her mother, Merle could have a terrible temper when she wanted. She was "restrained" by the motherhood of the 1960s—expected to devote her time and energies fully to her young children—and any intellectual pursuit she had previously been on was dashed accordingly. It was very frustrating for her because her security was now basically at the mercy of my endeavors, and she often let me know this in so many words. But in the midst of our arguments on what I was doing, and what Merle thought I *should* be doing, I would find myself the sole defender of pursuing the arts, of chasing a dream—and this actually strengthened my resolve.

I loved my family and appreciated them, but my heart just was not in the role of "household dad." I didn't dwell on singing the children to sleep or reading stories. When I woke up in the morning, my first thought was on securing an acting job. I just knew it was only a matter of time—it had to be. I had already given what I thought was so much; I knew what I was willing to give. So I weathered our sometimes explosive arguments, put my head down, fulfilled my substitute teaching obligations, and looked for something, anything to come along.

Some several months later, the same stage manager who had sent me to the pavement apparently mentioned my name to a producer as a replacement and I got into *Oliver!* In fact, one of the reasons I was chosen was because of my substitute teaching experience—the children playing Fagin's gang needing someone to keep their studies current while they were on the road. I had left a place for this, a darkening place made blacker by marital strife and sacrifice, and now I was on Broadway performing in the chorus of *Oliver!* It was almost surreal how quickly I picked it right back up, and I enjoyed myself immensely.

Then we took the show on the road. We were in Chicago, performing down in the theatre district and everything was going great, except for my family life back home. Merle, knowing how the theatre world *can be*—both people and short-term gigs—began to become very insecure that I was completely abandoning any intention of a stable, full-time job to support the family, and that I was using the opportunity to get away from our obviously strained relationship and carry on an affair with a member of the cast. She actually accused that this supposed affair was the reason I was so "difficult" toward her and was the main reason for our ongoing problems. She was left in that little apartment with two children, beholden to whatever she pieced together.

This wasn't good for her, wasn't good me, and wasn't good for the children—and I knew it. So I arranged for

Merle, and Rebecca, and Dominic Jr. to all come out to
Chicago and spend some time together as a family while I
was performing. Merle got to see firsthand that her suspi-
cions were unfounded—but this may not have helped as
much because it also confirmed just how much machinated
tension, fear, and anxiety had been left in that apartment
back home. But for the briefest of moments, I was an actor,
in a major production, supporting and surrounded by his
family; I had been given a glimpse.

When *Oliver!* ended, Merle dug in. Even though I immediately went back into substitute teaching and Folk City, it
wasn't enough of a commitment to family security for her. We
had some of our most famous "debates" about this. I smashed
my guitar to show how she was stabbing me in my soul. I just
couldn't believe that she would really ask me to give up my
art, especially after I had just proven that the next acting
job was never *too* far away. But we were sinking, and the only
thing that mattered in the world to Merle was my job stability.
Of course, to her credit, this was all compounded by the fact
that she was pregnant with our third child.

Then, I got another glimpse—kind of. It was November
9, 1965, and I was finally on the official performance card at
Folk City: my big debut. I had secured another guitar for the
time being and was rehearsing the few chords I knew all day.
I had a problem with singing and playing—it came across
rote—so I was very nervous and practiced up until around
5:30 p.m. that evening. All of a sudden all of the lights went
out, and Merle said, "Oh, our damn washing machine must

have short-circuited the house." But that didn't seem right to me—it was a modest apartment but not shoddy—so I stepped outside and the entire street was dark.

And then, as I soon learned, the entire northeastern United States was dark—welcome to the blackout of 1965. I called over to Folk City and John, the bartender, told me he was sitting by candlelight with no customers. I was relieved of my unprepared duty; I could barely contain myself as I hung up the phone! The next day, my extra rehearsal time provided me with just enough of a serviceable performance—I really struggled with sounding natural when playing and singing— and most importantly, I "passed" in the eyes of the owners. I had survived the billing thanks to a freak-nature, circum- stance-induced extra day of practicing and had experienced a "successful" folk performance. And soon after the lights came back on, our third child was born.

Sarah Francesca Chianese was born in 1966. Merle and I had our customary naming contention, and I walked away with "Francesca" as Sarah's middle name, after my grand- mother. I loved all of our children's names. Sarah's birth was a bright ray of light peering through our destructed rubble, and one that I wished had endured.

Saddled with three young children, living with Merle became almost unbearable. Every day spent substituting was really a "failure"; every stage-smile projected at Folk City was secretly shrouded in home-life turmoil; and every acting job that passed me up was just one more reminder of who I "really was." And somehow fate—or maybe it was something even more than fate—seeing the whole of this rapid and interminable decent, stepped in and intervened again, only this time with finality.

One day, like so many of the drab days that had blended together to really make just "one day," I came home from substitute teaching to find out that I'd received a phone call pertaining to an audition for *Sweet Chariot*, with Juliet Prowse, running in Las Vegas. Following up with this, I learned that the call had come personally from the stage manager, which meant I was pretty much being offered the role. Knowing that in this business, you're only as good as the next thing, I told Merle—with conviction—that I wanted to go. She hit the roof.

I had never seen Merle so mad, so upset. She stamped her foot and screamed—like her mother. "No! You can't do that. You can't do that!" Merle yelled, sending little four-year-old Rebecca cowering into the corner. It was completely crazy, this fury that had been unleashed.

I wanted to talk with her, to tell her how I wanted to quit teaching and go back into show business full-time, that I thought this was the break that would make that possible, and then, *then*, we could live the life we wanted. But she could not be reasoned with—not now, not ever. And I realized this would never change: Merle would never let me take the chance I needed to take in order to try and make it, in order to pursue my dream. I looked over at Rebecca huddled in the corner, trying to shield herself from this rage that I was at the center of. To go through these motions of "family," where ambitions are harbored, where contempt is constantly held; it wasn't fair to her, it wasn't fair to anyone. And in this realization, I suddenly understood that I had possessed the fortitude to do something I never thought I could. I left.

Chapter 5

PAT C.

It was raining. There was tremendous deafening thunder and hostile, excited, and desperate flashes. I needed to get somewhere quick because the storm was too much. I knew I wouldn't last; I got off the street just in time. And when the door closed behind me, it was almost surprising that nobody seemed to notice the catastrophic tirade taking place only a few feet away. Hammering boulders of piercing vitriolic resentment and family-tearing cries lay right outside.

In some shocked and reduced survival mode, I had fumbled over to Folk City. Mike Porco was there and let me convey the events while I stood on the precipice of complete abandonment and forced narrow solitude. I figured I could use nothing short of salvation at this point; Mike figured I could use a job.

Mike offered me the emcee position full-time, at a time when things over at Folk City weren't so copacetic either. The Vietnam draft was in full swing, and back home, folk music was on the front lines. I was thirty-four, so I didn't have to worry about immediate deployment, but hardly anyone got out unscathed, and I was incensed and involved regardless.

Ideals were evolving quickly, and an increasingly political audience was demanding a clear position be taken of its folk performers. Folk music was considered, very passionately by its respective audience, as a beaconing voice and key means of advancing a particular message. I was very apolitical to all of it—having been so taken aback and left in bewildered awe at the devastation of Hiroshima and Nagasaki—but, as a sometimes performer also, I was expected to fall into one of two camps: the obviously present anti-war and protesting folk singers, or the rampant patriots who espoused all things red, white, and blue, and left little room for a melting pot—much less the elbow room to stir it with.

Also brewing in this hornets' nest of live performance was the fact that singers, at the time, were very serious about the material they performed. That is, singers were not so readily switching formats or styles to conform to trends—at least not the dedicated singers who were taken seriously—and hopefully for them, they would land the "right" audience in this brooding scene. So when it came time for me to perform, I went with the international songs I knew and loved so much—the songs I knew would rise above the fray, much to my incorrect assessment.

"Now I'm going to sing you a song called 'Mi Caballo Blanco,'" I broadcast into the mic after having just played an Italian song. Then I got a request from one of Folk City's finer patrons, an ultimatum really. "Sing an *American* song!" some big guy draped over the jukebox yelled. What made the request all the more interesting was the fact that, at Folk City, the performing stage was only steps from the audience—a casually spoken song request would have been more than audible and sufficed just fine. But there had been a hasty inflection of tone, so the request was to be taken seriously. "Okay!" I acknowledged. "Here's a song from *South* America," I exclaimed as I began to sing "Mi Caballo Blanco."

It was about halfway through this fine patron's unswerving crusade toward the stage that I realized instant passion had not prompted him to jump up mid-song and grab an autograph. And because we were only several steps apart to begin with, I too had changed course mid-song and was now in my best batter's stance position, clutching my guitar, ready to send this fine patron—via swing—straight to Vietnam myself. But before I could give my encore of man-meets-guitar chordal emanations, the waiters piled on like a goal-line stand. This infuriated customer, who towered over most of us, who slowly dragged piled-on waiters one by one as he fulfilled his stage-bound manifest destiny, who at no point gave any indication of not killing me, was then "kindly" asked to leave. I couldn't believe I had been threatened for my art—I'd never even considered not singing what I wanted. This was America. I'd sing a Chinese song if I felt like it. I respected his right to be an American, but he had to respect mine too.

And it was in this swirling and toxigenic vociferousness that I could have very well and very easily escaped from myself and been swallowed whole, had it not been for the reality check of friends and family. Some of our mutual friends would frequent Folk City and say, "Oh, you should make up with Merle. You guys are good together." And I would tell them, "You live with her, not me, *you* live with her." She was not an easy person to live with, and apparently, neither was I.

Even my own mother and father could not understand why I didn't stick it out. It was almost unprecedented in our Italian culture to try and explain that traditional family life just wasn't fulfilling to me. I'd gone in with this notion that marriage was an institution that was solid and if two people really cared for each other, then they could always figure out along the way how to make it work. But Merle wasn't like my aunts, the daughters of immigrants, or even my sisters. She was a modern woman of the '60s who had her own agenda, and when my dream didn't align with her vision of my dream, she became very insecure for our family's future.

We were no longer the two up-and-coming actors having the coolest long-term fling down in the Village. Merle had wanted to have children right away, and once the children came, our passion-fueled romance was instantly traded in for the ever-sought peace and ease of steady hearth and home. And as far as Merle was concerned, my announced priorities for pursuing my dream of acting and performing—of which

I had been forthright with her and everyone in the beginning—were simultaneously traded in too. All support from
her now virtually ceased, and part of me was dying because I
needed theatre to sustain my soul.

I had grown attached to the camaraderie of the play,
the companionship, the friendship that ensued. Rehearsals
with specific casts could last for weeks, and in that time
artists would get to know one another, share enjoyable and
expected stories of oft puffed-up industry triumphs, and
invariably leave each other with a better sense of purpose:
the knowledge that there was more. Sometimes you would
work alongside actors, go your separate ways, and be recast
with them years later. It was an ongoing surrogate family, and
it was out there, and Merle and I used to chase it together.

But that seemed so long ago. And all I felt I had after
everything was to make a choice. And, as hard as it was, I
made an authentic choice. And I felt very guilty and very bad.
I'd chosen the unknown, and now I was alone. My one shred
of solace through it all was that I somehow didn't waver. I'd
chosen my dream.

Things were not just going to go away because I had,
however. Merle was furious that I had the nerve to leave her.
She had her brother Johnny drop by Folk City, and he was
steaming too. "What are you doing? What are you doing!?"
he demanded. "What I had to," I remorsefully told him. But
he wanted to fight. "Get away from me!" I would yell while
pressing on, reliving wounds. I had expected there would be
pushback, not necessarily to this degree, but pushback—but

nothing had prepared me for the devastation of Merle's mother.

Just because Merle and I couldn't live together didn't mean I considered myself absolved as a father. I loved our children—and did care for Merle, I just couldn't live with her—and I wanted very much to still be in our children's lives as much as I could, especially in these early formative years. So I tried to visit them.

I knocked on the apartment door and there was no answer. I continued to knock, hearing their young voices right on the other side, but no answer. Never had I even begun to fathom that our children would be used as a leverage point—there was just too much mutual love for them—and I let this thought echo as I tried to take the iron door down. And while I was railing on this entryway that now served as my paternal barrier, the pressing acknowledgment of my hoarded children growing more immense and more immediate, two cops, guns drawn, came out of nowhere. I explained that all I wanted to do was see my children, that we were barely even separated. So they got me in, but Merle wasn't there. And Sima was. She had hidden all three children in the midst of this, and these young children, who didn't know what was going on and why they were a part of it, were very frightened and very upset.

It was heart wrenching, this broken family I had created. And now the children were paying the price for a lack of cohesion. The regret and shame took equal turns on my scale of emotions, guilt already having heavily weighed in. I thought about going back. But I knew it was not going to work. There was too much animosity that could never be overcome by soulless diligence. Merle was a good mother, and I knew the children would be all right—perhaps even better off, if they didn't have to watch me surrender every night.

My consolation through all of this was my guitar. When I first started at Folk City, I only knew a few chords—but now that I had the full-time job, I was determined to really learn how to play. Through this truly wonderful instrument, I refocused and found my artistic drive while the world fell around me. I was determined that this was going to be my life.

My Folk City job also helped me to sustain and keep afloat. When I wasn't performing, which was most of the time, I actually got to meet some very interesting people. I introduced John Lee Hooker, Sonny Terry and Brownie McGhee, Arlo Guthrie, Dave Bromberg, and Roosevelt Sykes. I got to meet Judy Collins when she was young. And Simon and Garfunkel came through; *Sounds of Silence* was being recorded that year. Hundreds of talented artists took the stage at Gerde's Folk City, and little by little, this absorption of the artistic world that I held so near and dear began to bring me back from the brink. Then, the always-reliable American Library Association stepped in and turned things up a notch.

One evening, as I was completing my nightly emcee duties at Folk City, and after a particularly rocking performance by an unarguably promising jug band, I was approached by a lingering customer. The customer leaned in: "Dominic, we just came in from the Folger Library in Washington, DC.

The American Library Association's having a meeting in New York, and we'd love to hire you to put on a show for us. And if you can get the jug band that was on tonight, that would be great."

I happened to know the front man of the Dirdy Birdies Jug Band, Jack Pignatello, very well, so I said, "All right we'll put 'em all together." And we made up a price, and I arranged this deal: the jug band would perform and I would sing with female folk singer Jean Richards accompanying as well. Everything was set, and I was kind of proud of myself for handling this "business side" of show business, my first real experience in the driver's seat. The library guy seemed pleased enough also, and while he was leaving he turned and said, "Oh, by the way, if you could manage to get some go-go girls, that would be great. We'd really like to have some go-go girls."

Now, I realized this was 1966, and I had always left the door open to some of these library people amongst us really being party animals in recluse, but I honestly did not know where to round up said girls. So, disappointed at the potential deal breaker, I explained with heavy heart that I didn't know any go-go girls. He quickly responded, "I think we have some go-go girls who would like to work on it." These library people were adamant that girls were going to dance while they memorialized checking out books.

So we did the show and I relegated these library-sponsored girls to stage left and stage right, putting each of them up on a pedestal as if they were statues dedicated to good reads. I carefully explained, "Every once in a while, you gotta shake it and that's it." And one of the girls came over and said, "I'm not getting enough to do. Don't you think I should do more dancing?"

And I said, "Listen, this is a folk show. It's for the American Library Association. There's a jug band. And Jean Richards and I sing romantic songs...I don't think so." She told me she wanted more to do, and I told her, "I'm the director, and that's what you're gonna do." I actually enjoyed leading a show like that—even if it was under the somewhat bizarre circumstances that it was currently under—and I took note that I liked showing talent from behind the scenes as well, as the members of the American Library Association feasted upon the always-tantalizing, insatiably provocative book-praising, folk-dancing girls.

My approach was getting sharper; the artist in me was taking hold. I got a job as an understudy in *America Hurrah*. I had to learn the lines and cover three different guys in the show, but I was ready. I was succeeding as both an emcee and a performer at Folk City; my guitar playing kept getting better. *Man of La Mancha* was playing right across the street and someone from the show's crew complimented that I looked like Don Quixote—a role I had always wanted to play, and at this rate I figured it was only a matter of time. I breathed a *huge* sigh of relief that at least one of my unbearable burdens had been severely eased. While it wasn't all leading material, I could honestly say that I was working in show business.

Riding this lost high that I had once long ago known, I decided I would also partake in the mid-'60s and ease up on myself a little. After all, what good is living in the "scene" if you aren't really living? So I invited my family to come down and see my new-and-improved, fresh-on-the-show-business-wagon of a performance now playing at Folk City. Though my family was still highly reluctant to condone my actions with Merle and the children, they wanted to see me succeed, and their presence was more than enough of the blessing I was looking for to keep heading in—what I was hoping was—the right direction.

During the intermission, I was talking to my mother when I felt a tap on my shoulder. I turned around and was taken by the eyes of a stranger. The words "I want you" carried to my ears only, the low, sultry rasp imploring serious consideration. And my mother asked, "Who's that woman?" I told her I didn't know—and from the looks of the young woman, not many people really did. I was feeling pretty good about how the show was going, and my family was here to see me succeed, so I just chalked the whole thing up to the 1960s and finished out the set.

It was funny: I was getting back to firm footing art-wise; I had gotten my family to at least come down and support me in my new endeavor, of which they seemed to truly enjoy themselves; yet the thing I kept coming back to was: "I want you." And maybe, after my family congratulated me, said their goodbyes, and left, I hung around just a little longer than usual, just to see what might happen. The mysterious woman did too, and she gave me her phone number.

We were in her apartment, after seeing each other on several occasions, when her doorbell rang. "Don't move, I'll take care of it," she quickly stated. And she must have instantly identified her visitor because she immediately followed with, "Whatever you do, don't come to the door. Don't confront this person. He has a gun."

I had no idea who this girl was and what I was involved in. So I stayed down and tried to discern whatever conversation from the two of them I could while she stepped outside—as if my life depended it, because it sounded like it might. I couldn't really make out what they were saying, but I could tell from the guy's tone that he wasn't a practicing minister. When his voice trailed off I surmised that he had left, and she reentered, shaken up. She assured me that everything was okay now. I somehow did not fully believe it.

Knowing what I thought might be the case—and if so, she would be even more apprehensive when prodded—I put together a few carefully worded questions and pretty much confirmed what I had suspected: the guy who had visited was, in all likelihood, mob-connected. I also knew how this tale of "the mysterious woman and the new guy" could unfold, and I broke it off cold with her on the spot. She was infuriated that I would do that, especially after she had just "handled" everything, but I figured easily better her than the other guy.

I went back to my establishing routine of emceeing, performing, and part-time acting, when one evening before I went on stage at Folk City, the mysterious woman appeared again. She walked over, partially veiled in the darkness of half stage light, and whispered in her low, sultry rasp once more: "I ought to throw acid in your face." I didn't know what to do. I really didn't even know who this woman really was. It was just my time to perform. So I got up to go on stage, and thankfully walked out of her life for good.

Besides, I was now a full-time artist once again and there was a fresh, young artist down at Folk City who had been checking me out. Here sat this beautiful, full-bodied Norwegian, breezed in from Seattle, wearing smocks and clogs and igniting all conversations of painting and sculpting: the "scene" herself of the scene I was trying to live in—the embodiment of escape which I already did. She had an apartment and I was basically rootless, so it all worked out well.

Part of the reason I could get involved so easily is because, really, I wasn't. This was the "swinging '60s" I would tell myself as I looked to soothe the deep hurt I felt responsible for with surface-level encounters. And since all of these determinedly "meaningless" relationships were born of—from what seemed to be in my perspective—one of the epicenters of this whole counterculture, surely the women always felt the same way too. So it was no small surprise when I learned that Pat Crum, my awesome little Seattle hipster girlfriend, who had momentarily let me dock with her in a foul-smelling basement apartment while we both just happened to intersect journeys on this collectively named and independently traveled blinded risk we called life, told her family that we were married.

Now I knew it was over. Even the mere thought of anything beyond dalliance was just too much for me to bear. It reminded me of what I had done, of who I had done it to. It reminded me of who I was.

But Pat was in a bad place too. Her father had just passed in the midst of this marital charade, and I felt bad that I was only making things worse by letting her know I was out the door. There was almost a mutual understanding that Pat had made a mistake, and I "owed" her, one last time, for our uncommitted time together. So I agreed to travel to Seattle with her for the funeral, figuring that I would help her in her greatest time of need and at least try the role "on" once before taking my final bow.

Our last night together felt almost obligatory. I just wanted out of the whole thing but felt, having come this far, that— particularly given Pat's state—the legacy of Pat and I deserved the ribbon-bowed adornment of a quaint and mildly weird 1960s fling. Thus, we had one more night together: a way for two parting vessels to acknowledge a happenstance coalescence at confused and upset crossroads, a way to further achieve the era from which it had lived, a way to give hope that maybe it was more than it seemed. And afterward, we soon received finite definition to our unexpected, rough-and-tumble time together: Pat learned that she was pregnant.

In a way, I thought I had been trapped. Here I was, minding my own business, just going with whatever came my way, and this sculptor from Seattle, who may have very well hiked up to New York in clogs, for all I knew how they did things in

Seattle, staked me out at my performances, invited me to live with her knowing that I had nowhere to go, and delayed our inevitable split by claiming, in a time of need no less, that we were hitched, keeping me "on board"—out of the *goodness* of my heart—for the extra amount of time it took her to get pregnant. At least, that's the way I saw it. Being that I already had three children I could barely support, and knowing that Pat did have other male friends, my reaction to Pat's news may have caused her to see it differently.

Pat was honest enough. But I just couldn't get involved; I didn't want to. And as long as I held on to the fact that I knew she had other male friends, I could look the other way and maybe it would somehow all go away. She would continually tell me I was the father while I attempted to live external to the desperation. She called me once from a pay phone, further into her pregnancy, pleading with me, begging, "It's your child"—her neglected cries and isolated echoes embedding into phone booth walls. I could only bring myself to listen and exist inside apart—as distant as possible to come across, but really hand in hand in our descent.

Lea Chianese was born January 8, 1968, and when the time came, I willingly accepted her as mine. I actually had to go before a judge and tell him she was my child. But the judge, knowing my situation with my other three children, said, "Wait a minute, let's figure this out." But I insisted that she was my child. And she was. In spite of everything I had put Pat through, and all of the anguish I thought had been heaved onto me, there were a few moments of stillness when I held this precious baby girl, my newest and immediate center of pride and joy. And in these first few briefest of times with Lea, I found a respite—I found a quiet peace. Then Pat took Lea and went back to Seattle, and I never saw her again.

Alleviation came in acceptance. I convinced myself that I was after the intimacy a woman could provide me with, that I was lacking without. Whatever woman and forever how long that intimacy could be provided was exactly as it was intended. It didn't even take that much probing of depth, just a knowledge that this belief might possibly exist at my core. Things were moving fast, and as long as I didn't stop to think about it, I could justify moving on—a fathered child taken: the impression I had now paid all emotional tolls. Freed from the semblance of structure, I was a razor to my craft and my acting bled into my life. I played *myself* and only sought genuineness, yet lived capriciously. My actions were true to character, and hopefully this role wouldn't end.

I landed a part in a play and a new girlfriend at the same time. Adamantly scraping away at reeling loss with relentless ambition, I prioritized the two respectively. The play was *Jacobowski and the Colonel*, and I was playing a French policeman. Her name was Pat also; I didn't pause long enough to appreciate the substitutive irony; and it didn't last long. She was an apprentice with the production, and I regretfully wasn't very nice to her. She came at a time when I had much more stressful things on my mind: the play called for my character to ride a bike.

I had taken over the role for the actor Ed Grover—who had gone on to shoot a movie in California—and needed to learn the part in a short amount of time. The play was set in 1944 France and starred the great Yiddish vaudevillian Menasha Skulnik. It was a little intimidating, but the stage manager had faith. He said, "Dominic, I know you can do this. It's no problem. Just work on the monologue." So I worked on this fabled monologue in reference, this monster Shakespearian monologue that no mere mortal could wing. And after nailing this mouthful of hyperbole, this solo play of a monologue, this only foreseeable obstacle in the history of the production down in a matter of days, all I could think to say when I was told—before opening night—that I entered the scene on bike was: "What?!"

Having grown up in the jam-packed streets of New York City, and having been initially scared off by my mother's own fear-inspired tales of true wreck and abandon, I'd just happened to have missed my opportunity to learn bike riding. Fortunately for me, my options were very clear: face a childhood fear or sink the show. So, at thirty-seven years of age, I went out into the parking lot behind the theatre and used the final two hours before opening night to learn how to ride a bike.

The cue was an airplane. The production staff explained, "When you hear the airplane, the stage manager will hold back the curtain and you just ride in on the bike." *Just.* I sweated it out and *just* waited to ride; never mind the unabridged dictionary of a monologue I was juggling. All I was focusing on was the small miracle of maneuvering a bike twenty feet without anyone discovering my little secret.

The airplane came, *vrooooom*; the curtain went back, and I was off. The audience sat silently as I made my way steadily across the stage—an actor making a stage entrance to them, the most determined rider this side of the Tour de France to me. I kicked the stand and put it down: *whew!* I walked over to Menasha, got through everything, and the actress playing the French girl joined us as we all said "Vive la France!" It was incredible; it was triumphant—and the monologue was pretty good too. I had pulled it off! I could handle anything! Then, not necessarily designed to put a damper on the victory but more as a custom to these sorts of functions, we had another show the next night.

Vrooooom; I came out wiggly. That's okay, I told myself—no "gasps" from the audience were heard so no one probably noticed—just proceed as planned. I put the bike down and made my way to Menasha, but all I could think about was that entrance. I couldn't believe I'd blown it! Why hadn't this show been one night only?! And I was so consumed by this potential "career ender" that I just went over to Menasha and stood there. I had completely forgotten that in this particular scene, my character evidently was to recite some extended dialogue that I was to have prepared. And Menasha, the famous vaudevillian who knew how to work the stage, just looked at me too. Then, he looked at the audience and got a big laugh.

And this helped a little, and I eventually got through it, and at the end Menasha did another "take" to the audience like, "Who's this schmuck of a policeman?" getting another laugh and saving the whole thing. Then the French girl came out and kissed Menasha, we said "Vive la France," and I jumped back on the bike and zigzagged all over the place. The audience thought it was a circus act at this point. And while they were now most certainly waiting for the high-flying trapeze, I wobbled right into the curtain and knocked over the stage manager. The crew clamored, "Why didn't you tell us you couldn't ride a bike?!" Like I said: relentless ambition.

Menasha Skulnik, being the great, great man and performer that he was, sort of used that performance to set the tone for the rest of the show's run—playing fast and loose with the script. His wife, Rose, also a famous Yiddish vaudevillian, was cast in *Jacobowski and the Colonel* as well. And, of course, they had a great respect between them—but Rose would not let Menasha smoke cigarettes. He'd try and sneak them on break, and she'd come up and pull them right out of his hand. So one time, in one subsequent performance, he got his acting revenge.

In addition to playing the French policeman, I also had a small role as an old man in the first scene of the play. So, in this performance, we were into the opening scene and we had arrived to the point where Rose had a monologue—albeit not the encyclopedia with foreword edition of a monologue that had initially set us on this freewheeling path, but a monologue no less. And right as Rose was set to deliver this, Menasha skipped over it completely. He just jumped pages in the script for spite! And Rose was so upset about this, she broke character and came right over to me, in the middle of the performance, and said, in her true Yiddish accent, "You see vat he did to me! He cut the pages. You see how he is!" She was incredulously blazing; I didn't know what to say.

And when we performed in Philadelphia, Menasha struck again. Menasha was a smaller guy—he didn't stand more than 5' 2"—and there was a scene where he had to stand up to the big Polish colonel played by George Gaynes. So Gaynes, looking down at Menasha, issues his challenge. And because the play takes place in the 1940s, Menasha's character returns with, "In my veins flows the blood of great fighters. David..." and he mentions the names of all the great Jewish biblical heroes, and then Menasha added on his own, "*Moshe Dayan.*" And because the Six-Day War was still fresh in everyone's minds, and we were in a big city with an especially huge Jewish turnout in the audience that night, the whole place went nuts. He had actually ad-libbed and made it a richer experience. And it was times and experiences like these, of created, organic brilliance, and the surrounding of great people and professionals like Menasha Skulnik and Rose, that I was confirmed and substantiated in my knowledge that my only permanent relationship was with singing and acting—that show business was my most constant love.

But I was still emotionally needy. I was always looking for intimacy, a deep desire to be nurtured. Every woman I was with was a sincere attempt at a "fix"—my idea of the solution to what I thought the brokenness was.

I met a girl while we were in Philadelphia. She was a stage manager, and I couldn't *be with her*. My body began to reject what my heart thought it craved. I went to the Actors' Equity doctor and he gave me a pill that turned out a placebo. It was all in my head; the guilt sheared off as I fled to New York.

Comfort and friendliness: I awaited at Roslyn's door. An older, out-of-work actress who hung around the scene, she also was known as "Mother" to actors who had trouble staying between the lines. Begging for reprieve I'd knock, and when she would answer, we'd immediately slip into our "roles" of enduring mom and misplaced son. Welcoming my personal decline with open arms, she would serve me tea and then the main course. None of this was going anywhere fast, and surely not where I was.

My self-prescribed salvation transformed me into a crazy French priest. I had appropriately secured the role in legendary producer David Merrick's *Mata Hari*, and we were running a pre-Broadway tryout down in DC—back when they still did such a thing. Between the über-spirituality of my character, Maurice; the had-to-be-palpable psychic energy the 1960s induced me and my new psychically connected girlfriend, Carol, to believe we existed through; and my more than willingness to arrive at anything but the truth; I teetered on the edge of some self-envisioned nether region where the answer lay just short of "out there."

I was so wrapped up in this idea of savior-soul mate that I barely had time to be bothered while the show flopped all around me. Chalet pieces would fall and almost crush actors.

Actors would scratch their nose after they'd been shot. And Mata Hari herself even lost her dress one night. When I walked out of the National Theatre once after one of these rousing rehearsals, I noticed that the trees were filled with chirping blackbirds. I said, "Listen, Mr. Merrick! Those are the critics chirping!" And Merrick said, "I think this role is going to your head Dominic"—because I was the crazy priest. And the show did end up tanking because Merrick wanted to make it funny, and the creators unwisely made it serious. But I didn't really care. The thing fell to pieces on a nightly basis; I'd been waiting for them to join my party.

And just before the whole production imploded to the costly tune of two million dollars, I snatched this blonde singer who served up sexy psyche, who was hiding out from her boyfriend or husband—it really didn't matter—and stashed her away in a slapdash sublet I hurriedly arranged from my actor-buddy George. The only plan was that there wouldn't be one, that this thing could go as far as we could. But I also believed that what came was genuine, and the fall was so hard that I literally hit the ground.

I lay down on the floor. I did not feel well. I told Carol I really thought I was hearing voices. And even though we were casually walking through metaphysical doors together, my sickly proclamation really upset Carol. We got into a terrible fight about it; it almost got physical. She soon went back to whomever she left, and I was stalled in my angered state.

Carol was the first working professional actress that I had been with, and "all" that we had "been through"—as

I perceived—existed on common ground. If we weren't connecting professionally, it was at some interconnected soul juncture where held eye contact constituted a "higher level." And just as I had begun to finally sit down and have my slice of flower power to its fullest extent, the escape was taken from me.

It was very close to maddening. I couldn't be without a woman because I was too needy, yet when I was with women I pushed them to produce something they couldn't give. And somehow, through it all, I had still managed to establish myself as an at least credible actor and performer, the callousness of my past reinforcing my purpose. All I needed now was that final "something," that final someone who would help push me to success, to where I could really live for my art. I wanted someone who would encourage me to go on, someone who would say, "You can make it, don't worry. You can make it. Here's what we'll do. This is what we'll do to survive." I needed to find a woman who would be there for all of it. I needed to find a woman who would have as much craziness as I did to see this thing through. It turns out, she existed.

Chapter 6

LISSA HOLLOWAY

When the harmonies of two singers exist purely to complement each other's attunement, the only question that remains is, "Just *how* beautiful is this duet?" I had her. She was mine. This was going to work.

I was very fortunate to have plucked this premature angel from the late-'60s sonic wonderland known as Vermont; these heavenly seraphs were still earning their wings. *The* Maria von Trapp ran a lodge and restaurant on a gorgeous spread across mountainous Stowe—the hearkening of Austria drawing celestials near.

Two rabbis approached me and stated, "Ve like the vay you're doing Fagin. You're making him nice." I was nestled in the valley for summer stock's *Oliver!* and appreciated the compliments, knowing they worried I would play him dark. "You're a good boy. You're a good boy," one of the rabbis assured me in his old-country accent—the promising trajectory of his acknowledgment, my insular guide against ridgeline walls.

It was only a matter of time before I met the very young Lissa Holloway. She was in her early twenties and worked and sang at the Trapp Family Lodge, and we would sing *together*. Together. She wanted to be with me.

And when summer stock ended, I promised I would help her find an apartment in New York. Then I moved in with her. We were very much in love.

Lissa was one of the few women who my parents actually liked. Everybody liked her. She met my children, and they liked her. She didn't care that I had been married, and she would never mention it for us. Our relationship was everything, and we hushed and cradled it—not wanting to awake this delicate babe.

I had to lay down again, but this time it was different. This time I had Lissa. I had terrible aches and reached out to a friend's dentist, whose two questions for diagnosis were: "How old are you?" and "Where's the pain?" I told him I was thirty-seven and it was my chest, and he said it could be *it*.

It would seem that even the recipient of the direst disclosure could at least enjoy it with their last grain of salt—not forgetting that the bearer of demise was ultimately their friend's orthodontist. But, I had been accomplishing well-received dramatic performances as of late, and—having established a credible and natural knack for the theatrics—upon hearing the mere mention of such things as "heart attack," I completely freaked out.

Lissa was so worried that she rushed me over to the emergency room at Saint Vincent's Hospital without even questioning it. I didn't know what was going on—only that an actor I knew had referred me to his dentist when I had asked for a "doctor," and certain doom had been clearly spelled out from the subsequent Spanish Inquisition of a phone call medical examination.

On top of my final minutes passing by like the nurses who skipped me over for three hours, some poor guy who only spoke Mandarin was in the hospital bed next to me whining either about his indecipherable condition or the fact that Chinese was easier to learn than English. After a couple hours of poking the guy like he was a slow-cooking meat, somebody figured they'd had enough, the poor guy was "done" and did have appendicitis; and an entire medical staff with instant availability formed up, swooped in, and wheeled the fated patient to the great beyond: the next waiting area. Then, a doctor showed up, asked me if I was on drugs, and since I didn't respond with "best places to score," he told me I had the flu.

As nurturing and caring as Lissa was, she was equally, if not more so, supportive of my acting career. She never urged me to get a day job. She was with me all throughout summer stock and later that year, when I played seven characters in an Off-Broadway production called *Ballad for a Firing Squad* down at the Theatre de Lys in the Village. Lissa was becoming the Village girl that I had always wanted, the one who wanted it for me. Life now practically implored me to partake, but its unfamiliar rosy scent bred whimsicality at every turn.

My first run-in was with the accountant of *Ballad for a Firing Squad*. On the way to the show's final rehearsals, I met a man who told me he was the accountant who was on his way to see the show's producers—fair enough, I pointed him in the right direction. A week later, after the show was up and running, I saw Anne Bancroft and Frank Langella standing in the lobby after that day's matinee. I went over and introduced myself, and the accountant happened to be standing there as well. Politely, I turned and said, "Didn't I already meet you? You're the accountant, right?" And he stared straight at me and said, "No, I'm Mel Brooks. I'm famous." Everyone cracked up, and it started to feel like home.

I also happened to see a great show at the time, *Jacques Brel Is Alive and Well and Living in Paris*, and I decided I wanted to try and get in. The show was stacked with some twenty-five-plus songs. It was a music lover's dream, and with Lissa's encouragement, it was mine.

Most of my time was devoted to learning this behemoth songbook and trying to get into the show. And after three or four auditions, they eventually hired me on. As part of the substitute ensemble, I stayed ready to jump in if any of the main performers dropped out of the show, and the substitutes were collectively given certain matinee performances to headline every now and then as well. I was coming up the way I had always wanted: I had the job, I had the girl, I finally had it all—even my very own musical nemesis.

It was somewhat of a small and monumental personal victory to have learned almost thirty songs within a few weeks. But there was one song that I just could not quite get: "Fanette." For some reason, it seemed the song had an obscure timing change at the end of it; and partly because I had never really learned music intrinsically, as opposed to some of the rote memorization I had relied upon in the past, I was always slightly off on this one song. And because we were flying through this whirlwind cacophony songbook in what little time-crunched rehearsals we had, the staff never obliged my request for extra practice with the lurking nemesis.

Now, it would seem that there are a couple of things—with reliable certitude—to be counted on when dealing with a nemesis: it will strike, and it never works alone. Having performed on a variety of stage types and in numerous performance halls, I can attest that stage dimensions usually come in the "arc," the "rectangle," or the "hexagonal" shapes. The Village Gate on Bleecker Street, where we performed *Jacques Brel Is Alive and Well and Living in Paris,* had a performance space that was none of these. It turned out that this was a very key piece of information to know up front because having a reliable stage type is especially important when an actor is performing and doing other things simultaneously, such as trying to go over an upcoming nemesis song within that very performance, and readjusting to the instant realization that the given actor's family has made a surprise visit to the day's performance and is now belting out comments from the back of the house.

For this specific performance, the staff had taken me up on my role of substitute and I was opening the show. So I came out to do the opening number, "Marieke"—a very strong opener in its own right—and the chasing spotlight was on. "There he is!" shouted someone from the audience as I carefully hid my apprehension to the possible familiarity of this matinee Paul Revere. And as I went by the well-rehearsed steps to this powerful song, the spotlight gave me the briefest of blinding reprieves, and I saw that it had been my Uncle Joe.

Falling back on duty and experience, I steadfastly completed the gripping intro, albeit with the pressing and incessant thought of "Oh great, my family's here"—never truly forgetting that the persisting breath on my neck was the hanging presence of "Fanette." And when the song ended, I let experience dictate my action again and guide me through this now-befuddling exit. However, because the segue music was so thunderous and all experience knew was the more traditional platform configurations, my clouded judgment forced me to take a step of faith, and I faithfully fell five feet off the stage and crashed through the table below.

Fortunately, this being a Sunday afternoon show, food and drinks were not served and the table to which I had now extended the performance was not being used. Otherwise, I might have even killed somebody. The stage lights came back up and another performer, a confused John Seattle, came out and drove diligently into the next song while watching me scramble back on stage—we had twenty more numbers to get through; you had no choice but to keep going!

Despite my best earlier efforts, *Jacques Brel Is Alive and Well and Living in Paris* became a cultural hit. The show was very controversial: it was very anti-war, anti-Vietnam. It quickly ascended to cult status.

And because of its timely popularity, I ended up performing in it for about a year. I would put my whole heart into the show, and the audience really seemed to enjoy my performance. The producers of the show arranged for the Washington, DC, performance to be held at Arena Stage, so I got to perform the bullfight song in an actual arena. It was a wonderful experience, and while it was still hard for me to step into my past and visit Rebecca, Dominic Jr., and Sarah in Brooklyn, I had enough of a good thing going to finally grind the lingering sadness to something bittersweet. I knew they were in good hands, and if everything worked out, I would be able to be the father that I wanted.

Lissa supported my every move. She championed me in my art. And it was with this peace and foresight that I welcomed a happiness I had not yet known—a happiness that it was acceptable to pursue my dream. Thus, this welcomed stranger "happiness," who knew no permanent abode, brought with it the expectancy unknown: the potential of the unproven path to venture toward something amiss.

"You're pretty good, aren't you?"

"Yeah, I *am* good"—with undoubted retort, "Why?" The *star* had returned.

Jacques Brel had always been an ensemble show in my mind. We had multiple performers moving in tandem, we did multiple songs, and we traversed multiple cities. Everyone got along well with each other: it was the shining example of the surrogate family I had known to await. But Elly Stone had come back, and in her mind, it was a star show—and she was the star.

Elly decided not to like me, and that's how she saw herself. She challenged my ability and seemed to resent that I was strictly, when it came to the show, all business—I would respectively receive my deepening applause at the end of the performance, then leave; I wouldn't hang around afterward like some of the younger actors and dress her in her daily schmooze. I was in my late thirties and had logged too many years to knowingly help people plan out their ego trips. So after Elly rejoined, and realized that her fawning would never be complete, she sought to have me extricated by the one and only credible means she had: my nemesis.

Being that I was so well received amongst our ensemble, I was substituting for both male roles. This meant more opportunities for "Fanette"—which meant opportunities for a thrown-off timing, which happened. Not to the extent of my literally smashing debut, but it did happen. I had practically begged for specific rehearsal time on that song, but it was methodically to no avail. And Elly used this fault to drive a permanent wedge between me and the show's producers. And because she was the casted "star," they fired me.

That's when I realized that the industry was no exception to life. There would always be those who would seek to minimize and diminish your talent if they perceived it as a threat to their personal gain. I realized that I had done nothing but the best job that I could, and there had been a conspiracy against that. And we were all susceptible, no matter how talented we were and how well we were received. I understood human nature just a little bit more, and I was saddened.

I had given my heart and soul to the show, and they did break one—but this time they couldn't have the other. I wasn't going to be made to feel insignificant. This time, I wouldn't fully surrender. I had come too far. I was too strong and confident in my ability now. I knew who I was as an actor. I had a girl that believed.

Yet, the funniest thing happened. When I came home, no one was there. At least, no one I knew.

Strife, pressure, and to a lesser degree responsibility were all absent and unaccounted for. This was what I knew of "failure," of disappointment—of walking off the stage and back into home life. These were the virtues I had lived with, from which my identity was painfully forged.

But Lissa changed all of that. She was unyieldingly supportive of my success's eventuality. Even if I had been technically fired for a performance shortcoming, in Lissa's mind, what did they know? She believed enough in me to know that I was closer than ever, that we were closer than ever.

This newly lacked resistance caught me completely off guard. I was out of balance when I walked in the door. Struggling to stand up as I thought I knew who I was, I frantically grabbed at anything to avoid another fall. I found guilt, and I stood tall.

I had done too much, to too many people. There was a structure that was born of my heritage, but that was a long time ago. This was a new world, and I had helped to make it, and now I was in it.

What Lissa offered was too pure, too true—how could I ever deserve this? It seemed deceptive in its simplicity: just take her hand, and her love would be enough. But I bore a heaviness that I could never get out from under. Lissa only saw the way forward; I saw the past.

I reached down inside and summoned a false strength; I did what *I* had to do. There was comfort in remissness, a security in denial. Lissa was waiting. She wanted me to come with her. But I had never known where we would be going, so I disavowed my worth; I turned away.

Jackie B. was soulful. She was a sexy Jewish actress and singer. She was around, and I was around, and she stayed at her friend's house—and sometimes I stayed with her. Reliable ways had brought me my *ace*, and I was freed up to maneuver around commitment's threshold.

Off-Broadway was quickly catching on and I was cast in Frank Gagliano's *City Scene* alongside Raul Julia and Terry Kiser. Michael Douglas was in it too—it was his first Off-Broadway play. It was actually two one-act plays about

New York, and the three of us had a blast doing it. In fact, I may have taken things too far, and when I went on stage *tight*—"since," I so wanted to justify, one play had not given me any lines—I could unavoidably tell I wasn't as sharp-minded as I believed my craft called for. So I promised myself that would be the last time I *ever* did anything to impair my performance. And it was.

The plays themselves were interesting in that they dealt with how New York was increasingly becoming grittier—and the ensuing "rising terror" that was now promptly associated with the city. The second production of the double bill, *City Scene II: Conerico Was Here to Stay*, was a very heavy play. Raul played a Puerto Rican killer, I played a wild subway-dwelling blind man, and Terry played the victim. And it was through the sharp commentary and heavy roles that I got a chance to see some of the new, up-and-coming talent firsthand. And more importantly, I got the chance to make the acquaintance of one of my greatest friends: Raul Julia.

Raul was a very spiritual person. He was always there for me. He'd have everyone over to his house and we would all talk, sing, and share food. He taught me how to sing "Guantanamera" with the right translated lyrics, and I'd repay him with Italian songs.

And while everybody would carry on and have a good time, Raul would continually raise the energy. He would instantly burst into musical improvisations complete with funny, wild, and seemingly outrageous singing in order to ensure his guests were highly entertained. And sometimes, where I could, I would join in too.

It always felt good to be in Raul's company. And when I unburdened my heart to him, he would always answer straight. He would tell me about destroying the mythologies that sometimes keep us down, about having self-confidence. He seemed to understand where I was coming from; he understood my pain. He learned from life and brought it into his art. He learned from art and brought it into his life.

Raul was a true actor because he knew the difference between the privilege of performance and the sheer joys of being a human being. If the acting community was a surrogate family, then Raul was a true family man. He lived life so brilliantly that his radiant glow reenergized the lives of those around him. I would have done anything for my friend, this real luminary; and as Raul would have it, I did.

He was just finalizing a divorce to his Puerto Rican wife, so he was going through some changes. But, being so full of life, once newly single, Raul was instantaneously drawn to a vibrant dancer named Merel Poloway. He lamented: "Dominic, this girl is beautiful and I don't know how to reach her."

But I did. I knew a mutual friend of Merel's: it was Jackie B. Privy to this small discovery, Raul had but two simple requests: kindly get word to Merel that he's irrevocably nuts about her, and for the love of everything sacred, get them introduced.

This took a little finessing, as Merel was reluctant to be involved with a newly divorced man. But, I knew that Raul would have done it for me, so I recruited Jackie for the cause and we laid it on thick enough to not only get them together but send them beelining toward the altar. Of course, Raul's humble and loving personality did most of the legwork. Then, when the smoke from Raul's newfound seventh heaven with Merel settled into the burning fire of glorious passion that was Raul's everyday routine, he had some matchmaking work for me.

I confessed to Raul that I was a man of two lovers, torn between the one who was true and the one who was there; I had all of these presuppositions carefully mapped out. I'd been on unsteady ground so many times before, I was cautious to make any moves. And Raul took everything in and laid it out very simple: just go with the heart. So with Raul's urging, I knew I had to make a choice between Lissa and Jackie, and I chose Lissa.

But even though I chose Lissa, I didn't actually *choose* her. I merely chose to keep the option open. I was approaching forty and when it came to love, all I had to look back on were two annulments and Merle—three failures from where I stood. I just didn't think I could bear one more, and I cared enough for Lissa to convince myself that I was sparing her by remaining "away." If I was to let go and accept what I really had, then I could see that we might go deeper than I ever had been. The problem was, I also could see who was captain of the ship.

The always-dependable summer stock offered my most hopeful back door. As long as I was away, then I could argue my right to be "away," and I could suspend the inevitable hurt: the hurt that what she gave was real—the cost of acceptance, I could never afford.

So it was down in Cockeysville that I found myself on the floor once more. I was cast as head villain Harry Roat in the intense thriller—titled much to the chagrin of my life's direction—*Wait Until Dark*; and unfortunately, the show's producers had also taken to the term literally.

Since the dawn of acting time, the successful idea for a typical dinner theatre, as this unpretentious dinner theatre bound to Baltimore's rim *appeared* inclusively to subscribe, was to host a leisurely, ample meal followed into the evening with lighter fare: namely a musical or comedy. However, this *was* 1969, and the show's producers were keeping with the culture—which, in the art world, was quickly becoming the counterculture, now apparently even purveyed at the modest playhouse level—and they decided that "tried and true" was far too vapid.

And though these cultural rebels of producers held the fort and offered their best efforts toward the advancement of "progress" at the outpost of Baltimore, in the end, a sole, dependable, timeless humankind attribute seemed to undermine it all: when you put a lot of food out without much restriction, some people will surely gorge.

Therefore, it was with this persisting truth that I watched it all unravel. We were into the scene where my character was weakened and desperately crawling on his elbows, trying to reach the blind girl, Susie, before she could uprightly defend herself and alert the cops. But I forgot to wear elbow pads—and I didn't want to halt the performance on my account—so I resorted to *method* and sincerely and painfully understood my character's physical struggle as I grinded it out across the hard stage floor. My selfless "act" was in vain, however, as the props guy had already made disrupting and final plans of his own.

Not to be content with just weeks of elbow damage, it seemed the props guy wanted to leave me with enough souvenirs to never forget why we stridently fought what worked so well in dinner theatre before. The moment called for a gunshot. And the props guy actually fired a gun in the enclosed space, puncturing my eardrum and sending the audience into a screaming frenzy. And because some of our instantly mortified patrons had justified that second or third helping of mashed potatoes with the assuredness that emotional heights of this level were unattainable for the duration of the evening, they threw up. Progress still had a ways to go.

I survived scathed and achieved my goal twofold: my performance was strong enough for next year's cordial invitation, and I was subsequently able to condition my relationship with Lissa as a committal challenge in the face of a reoccurring, momentum-blunting summer stock. At least, that was the theory; and it was under this alleviating and joyous theory that I returned the following year to even more success as Harry Berlin in *Luv*—the theatre itself also making a triumphant return by means of wisely showcasing a comedy—and I even decided that this time I would select my own remembrance of all of this generous *free* love.

Murray Schisgal's *Luv* provided one of the highlights of my stage career because the role of Harry was all comedy, all shtick. It was wholly rejuvenating to make the audience laugh again, to be a part of them really enjoying themselves—I was overwhelmingly received. And it was with the confidence of a jubilant audience's approval that I allowed myself to singly enjoy the moment: the freest raindrop on its way to the ocean, not knowing of its expanding world.

Existentialism. What is it about?

"I have no idea."

"Neither do I"—it was honest, and it was all I could think of.

These were philosophical and interesting times, and I was *interested*: not only in the book on existentialism that she was reading, but also in the liberating beauty of the green-eyed redhead herself. Normally, I never approached a woman without some sort of mutual agreement, but I was almost capsizing with glee between the very successful performance high I was still riding and the anticipatory potential that a train ride between two strangers on their way to New York instills.

So I struck up a conversation with her and found out the following: her name was Pam Bittner, she was heading back to New York after visiting her army-enlisted boyfriend in Baltimore, she wanted to be a dancer and was involved with a dancer-themed organization called the Rehearsal Club, and she was initially intrigued enough at my prospects of acting to turn our conversation into a full-fledged date, then more dates, then altogether leave her boyfriend—which she did.

"You can't have your cake and eat it too," Pop used to always tell me. But it seemed to me that I had found a way. Because I had met Pam during the newly established borders of the "summer months" between Lissa and I, these two relationships existed completely external, both physically and emotionally. That is, even though I would frequent New York off and on throughout the summer, it was understood by an emphatically supportive Lissa that I needed my creative freedom to fully absorb my work—that our time apart was next to nothing compared to what our time together would be once I was "somebody." So as long as I was "working" toward being this "whole person" who had finally made it, what difference did it matter if I had a little fun on the side? At least that's how I sold it; and I had to admit, this cake tasted pretty good.

And while I indulged in the many slices coming my way, I began to realize that maybe I was doing something right; maybe as long as I was putting my pursuit first, the natural extensions of everyday life—those that were more pertinent to the "real world," the world which Pop had known was calling, the world which I had known so cruel—would simply fall away unnecessarily, and I would be left with my righteous self.

Then I rightly let go with inhibition unbound. This was the time of Pam and me; this was the time of me. I was giving successful, highly praised performances. I was building up my acting reputation, which I knew would lead to greatness for all. I was getting what I needed from both women, and carefully keeping them exclusive—because I cared for them. I was well on my way to the person I was *so close* to being. I was doing it all on my own, but I was never alone.

There was no more reason to run, no more reason to hide. Those who needed to find me knew where to find me. I was holed up with Pam at my place down in Cockeysville, living my orchestrated life. Everything was being put in its place, my security masked as self-control. Speculation's window shuttered, and I charted the course of my jurisdiction.

It was poetically intoxicating, this vicious cycle: the way I masterfully extracted what I needed from all people and things, the way I gave just the right amount back. But just before the unknown vanquished and I was given definite hold, a beaming shapeless warmth took form and firmly waited at my door. Lissa had decided to pay me a surprise visit.

My art was my passion; my passion was what drove me. I had to satisfy my passion. Everything else was a substitute. I had no idea of the repercussions of my decisions, only that casualties could be necessary as I made *my* way. And she knew all of this. Lissa knew all of this about me, and still she had come. She was very much in love.

And as I saw the car pull up, and Lissa emerge while her grandmother waited, it was all so abundantly clear. Everything I really needed lay just outside of my door. Her love was so persistent; there was nowhere I could turn. There would be nothing that I could do to ever make it go. And with each pressing of the doorbell, each ringing acknowledgment of life passing me by, I accepted a little more what I already knew: I could never have a love so real, the only love that is. It was untainted and would always be. It was unconditional.

Chapter 7

PAM

Darkness had arrived. The first time I encountered it, it scared the hell out of me.

One of the ways I first made myself susceptible was through my vigorously determined treks to discover the unabashed secrets comprising a world called "real," the constitution of which namely existing as half-mile hikes to DC's local Sylvan Theater—an actualized quest "grand," the payoff even grander.

Having traversed and overcome immeasurable odds, at least from a ten-year-old's perspective, I would rightly plop down in the movie seats and await the important informational update on how the world outside my household had been fairing and hopefully progressing—known collectively as a "movie" to the abled and vetted ticket buyer like myself, now obliged to settle in, a man of the world amongst fellow men: the few, the bold, the early matinee ticketholders.

I had always suspected that it existed: a place where dreams really did come to life, the place where imagination was key. Bereft of mandated "growth" for a couple of hours, I fully absorbed the unprecedented possibilities—an eagerness kept voraciously fed by countless examples of seeming limitlessness. My idols would light up the screen and I would be awed and amazed and, even back then, motivated. When Bing Crosby sang "I'm dreaming of a white Christmas" in *White Christmas,* I felt we had reached a new cultural touchstone. At least, I know I did. And though these short-lived ecstasies would inescapably come to a close, their upbeat promises of endless joy ceaselessly carried on.

But one time I diverted from all things saccharine, and a virgin youth was left with nowhere to turn. This time I ventured into something different; this time I saw *The Devil and Daniel Webster.* And as enthralling as reaching up to the box office and securing a pass to such a provocatively titled feature was for a child in 1941, nothing prepared me for the devastatingly unnerving experience that waited just inside.

Acting largely incorporates the ability to use memories and then recreate them: to utilize a creative and active imagination—Walt Witcover and Bernie Barrow taught me as much. You have to be able to activate specific memories, while staying true to the character in the moment, so that the line and action will come out in the intended way. It's like peeling an onion to get to the heart of the character,

136

and when you reach a certain depth, you have your strongest memories to guide you.

So when my agent, the hardworking and dependable Jeff Hunter, phoned me to inform that a part in Archibald MacLeish's *Scratch*—based on *The Devil and Daniel Webster*—had opened up for a showcase in Boston, I immediately recalled the still terrifying and haunting image of Walter Huston as the Devil himself, stepping out of the fireplace in *The Devil and Daniel Webster*, which had petrified me as a child. Knowing how I could play the jury member who "comes in from the underworld," I told Jeff, "Sure!"

It was a beautiful play. And even though I didn't have any lines, I was really learning my craft. I got to work with one of my acting idols, Will Geer. And of course, Archibald MacLeish himself was there. And the great makeup artist, Joseph Cranzano, was also involved with the production and showed us how to expertly apply makeup—the importance and significance of which I appreciated even more so through my nonspeaking role.

My acting life was coming together; I was melding technique and experience into a formidable product. On the stage, I was mastering my domain, able to live in the character moment to moment. But in my real life, I could never capture that. In my own life, I was barely hanging on by impulse.

There was a party after one of the performances one evening, and Archibald MacLeish made it a point—despite that, days previous, I had unknowingly ushered him around a labyrinth of backstage corridors and stairwells and into the men's room, when he had simply requested guidance to the stage manager's office—to come over and congratulate us personally. Pam was wearing her green dress, and she was pregnant.

We were all very excited. And then Jeff Hunter called, and he was excited too.

Apparently, I had been selected for a follow-up reading in New York to some movie in the works called *The Godfather*. There weren't too many established stars attached to the picture at the time so who knew how far that would go; I was already in the middle of a great production, was getting good experience, and had done little screen work anyway; and Pam was pregnant; so I remained a stalwart to my misplaced stability, indomitable to my impulsive cause. I told Jeff no, I'm not coming down. I tremendously blew off *The Godfather*.

Career plan firmly in tow, I completed the show's run and headed back to New York on my *own* terms. Then, at the apartment Pam and I shared on 69th Street, I received another phone call—albeit slightly more sobering than the last one.

"By the way, our divorce finally went through."

"Oh fine, good," I casually mustered. Although Merle and I had split up in 1966, it wasn't until 1971 that it became legal—five years hindered because I couldn't bring myself to handle bureaucracies and the full responsibilities of a mature person, a process moving like clockwork by all of my accounts.

I hung up the phone with Merle and made another sudden decision: I could work my way out if I just did the *right* thing. So I called up Raul Julia and told him I wanted our baby to be born under Pam's mother's good graces. Raul was in bed and very sick but didn't hesitate for a second in agreeing that he and his wife, Merel, would witness my soon-to-be-within-a-matter-of-minutes holy matrimony down at city hall.

Pam grabbed her green dress and we ran—as best as we could, under the circumstances that Pam could give birth literally at any second—downtown to declare our burning love. And when the judge looked out and asked the whole congregation of all four of us, "If anyone has anything against this marriage, speak now or forever hold it," I remembered thinking about how it must look to be asking this question to a very pregnant Pam, a very sick Raul Julia, a very supportive Merel, and the impulsive exemplar himself; and how the only holding about to take place was a newborn in the judge's arms if he didn't hurry up and finish the proceedings.

Alex Chianese was born four days later, on August 17, 1971. And while it was a very special and joyful occasion, it was also a very difficult time—especially financially.

Acting work wasn't steady or supportive, and I was down to performing at a saloon on 65th Street, playing my guitar for cash tips. I was barely scraping by on the rent and didn't even have enough for diapers—let alone the support I was supposed to be paying Merle. At one point, it got so dire that I had to swallow my pride and ask the nice little white-haired old lady at the Actors Fund for a handout. Our common bond of theatre masked how far apart our worlds really were, and when she retrieved a gift of twenty dollars I reflected on my shortcomings and cried.

But I had persevered long enough to at least be known within the industry. During one of my "last stand" performances down at the saloon, I received a phone call from Sylvia Fay, a prominent casting director who was known for casting background players in television and film. She said, "Dominic, I'm going to send you to Boston. They want you to do this walk-on in a movie called *Fuzz*. Do you have the money to get there?"

According to my tip jar, the answer was "no," so I told Sylvia I would ask the bartender. And in another fell swoop of prowess on the business side of things, I arranged for the owner-bartender to loan me thirty bucks for bus fare, knowing that I would pay it back as soon as I returned from my first-ever paying film role.

I went up to Boston, said my one line, "Hey brother, can you spare a dime?"—which was deliberately shot in the dark—returned home, repaid the bartender, and went about as if nothing really happened. Shortly thereafter, I received a Christmas card from Burt Reynolds. I thought to myself: "*Who the heck is Burt Reynolds?*" Then it dawned on me: I had been so far removed from the central production of *Fuzz* that I didn't realize he was the star!

It was good to have finally broken into film, but from where I stood the outlook was bleak. I had already seen one family dissolve in the wake of an adamant dream, and I knew Pam and I weren't going to get far on performances that led to bus tickets. In a way, our hardships offered a second chance: I could make good on our vows; I could do right by my family—I could become the expected average working dad. So with barely any need to talk myself into it, I put away this crazy notion of "actor-father" and went straight from the big screen to the drug screen: I accepted a full-time, dream-shelving job with the New York Drug and Alcohol Commission.

And truthfully, it wasn't all that bad. I would go into the rehab center for young women over on 42nd Street and teach everyone guitar and participate in recreational activities with them—the lighter side of life for the mostly minority group of women who collectively ran the gamut on criminal records and mothered young. I liked them and they liked me; we got along very well. They would tease me about my "trendy" smoking habit, saying things like, "You been smoking marijuana, Dominic? Your fingers got all that tobacco on it." And I'd explain that it wasn't a result of absentness but more a product of nervous impulse—the two remaining not so dissimilar, the more time that we would all spend.

I had figured out a way for Pam and me to get by, but there wasn't room for much more. We would take little Alex down to Central Park and let him play to his heart's content, unbeknownst to him that it was all we could afford. And sometimes I would run into a fellow unknown struggling actor, a young John Lithgow, who would bring his son for the same reason too. We'd sit and talk while our children played, and I began to accept that this might work. I'd even run into Jackie B., who was always very sweet as she struggled in her acting as well. And as I was promoted in my nine-to-five while reminded of the realities to success, I understood what Pop might have been getting at: that there would always come a "time." I was a father *now*, and I wasn't the only one; and maybe dreams were only dreamt.

But while I was cozying up to this idea of a placid existence, the city itself was not. One time, after I had been walking with Pam and had briefly split off to go for an audition—because I enjoyed the scene and still kept the tip of my shoe in the door—Pam solely pushed Alex in his stroller across the always-sound Central Park. Upon exiting, though, she was more than stepping onto Central Park West at 69th Street: she was stepping into New York City in the 1970s, and the heat was turning up.

The policeman I found back at my apartment was more than happy to fill me in. As Pam had pushed Alex across the street, a man sprang forth, put his arm around her throat, and pressed her neck to his knife. Completely caught off guard, a terrified Pam involuntarily released the stroller and Alex rolled aimlessly into the street. Fortunately, the whole city hadn't flipped yet, and a random passerby intervened, yanking Alex out of incoming traffic.

Seizing her opportunity at this unexpected development of Alex's rescue within this criminal mastermind's plan, Pam did some kind of quick evasive movement—her sharp instincts and strength finely tuned from her experience as a dancer—and she immediately got between Alex and the thug. But the guy was a nut job; he just stood there. And this plain-clothes detective, who skimmed nothing from his recollected "divine intervention," just happened to be close enough for apprehension. But the way this cop told it in hindsight, you'd have thought he was preparing his interview for nightly newscast lead story contention. It was all about how he had "cleaned up the streets" with one last bad guy, as opposed to safely protecting a mother and her child. Pam was the one who could have been killed. She was the real hero.

It was horrendous for about a month and a half—*bureau-cracy at its finest.* The savior cop would drop by with questions and new ways of telling his criminal enterprise-blunting inter-cession. The DA's office would call and ask what *I* thought they should do. It turned out the guy had over thirty arrests and no convictions, so I told the DA to forget parole and go straight to hard time. Of course, in a backed-up justice system, that meant a couple of years.

The whole thing made me livid; I was shocked into a silent rage. I couldn't believe a known offender walked the streets and attacked women with babies. When I had to go down to the station with Pam for the assailant's identification, the cops were watching *me!* They must have seen the anger I harbored, the resentment I carried. They must have known about my unforgiving place.

I had to move on despite whatever I was suppressing; I had a job to do. I was a working dad. Pooling everything that

I could, I got Pam and Alex off the street and Alex into day care. And eventually I let the whole thing subside—at least at the surface—and began to acclimate again to the daily "life."

It wasn't so bad, and the good always came with the bad, right? And I even began to take Alex back into the park where we could once again watch the days go by. Then, in one of our chance and friendly meetings, Jackie B. asked me a question:

"Dominic, what do you want out of life?"

I told her I just wanted to help people.

And she said, "I just want to create beauty."

But she died very soon thereafter in a horrible elevator accident. When I heard about the terrible news from Merel Poloway, it was very upsetting. Raul and Merel went to her funeral; I was married to Pam, so I sent flowers. And just as I had begun to comfortably accept the limited potential of my self-sustaining routine, one of life's most sweet and welcomed pleasantries was taken away, revealing just how unhappy I really was.

So it was with no small fortune when my phone rang once more.

"Dominic, they want you for *Godfather II.*"

Jeff Hunter: the hardest working agent in the business, as far as I was concerned. *The Godfather* had been an enormous hit, and the same talented principal cast was returning, so it stood to reason that the sequel would be something of a blockbuster. This time, I managed to dig down deep and summon my most cunning and shrewd discernment ability; this time I had the common sense to say "yes."

It seemed that everything turned on a dime. Even Pam was excited about it. She said, "You deserve this, you know"— which was more than I needed to hear. I immediately quit my job at the Drug and Alcohol Commission and we all jumped on the first jet—not the smallest feat considering Pam was pregnant again—to Lake Tahoe, where they were starting to shoot.

Francis Ford Coppola told me, "You know, we wanted you for *The Godfather*. We were considering you for Sollozzo, the Turk." He's the one with the police captain in the first *Godfather* who gets shot at the restaurant. But they had kept me in mind for *The Godfather: Part II*, and I ended up getting as good a part, if not a better one. Thank goodness Francis had a good memory and didn't hold any grudges!

So here I was, all of sudden sitting with Al Pacino, being directed by Francis Coppola, playing the gangster Johnny Ola—who was actually based on real-life gangster Vincent "Jimmy Blue Eyes" Alo, who himself had grown up on the Lower East Side.

And we were shooting the crucial scene where I tell Pacino, in essence: *Hyman Roth wants to work with you, and we'll take care of everything. Hyman Roth always makes money for his partners, and we'll help you get into the gambling business. Hyman Roth is on your side—that's why I'm here.* So I had to deliver the information very carefully, knowing that Johnny Ola knew the Corleone family did not trust Hyman Roth's gang—Roth being heavily connected with the Corleone's adversaries.

I also had to be aware that Johnny Ola knew that Roth's people were really out to betray the Corleones, and I was the one guy who could deliver the message because Johnny had known Michael Corleone since they were kids. And Michael was the new young leader of the Corleone family—so this was a very important speech I had to deliver. And as I entered the room and sat down and began the speech explaining how Roth was really in cahoots with them, Coppola interrupted me and said, "Dominic, I realize now that I want to change the name of the lawyer. Instead of Green, say Brown."

"All right," I said.

Camera. Action.

By this time, even though it was my first real film role, I'd had over twenty-five years of acting experience: I knew my monologue. So when Francis mentioned this slight name change, I instantly acknowledged—a minor change, business as usual. Facing Al in the chair, I looked into his eyes—Johnny needing to gain trust—and he looked back—potentially reciprocating the sentiment—and I deftly got through the speech all the way up until the point of the name change, and then I forgot it.

I stopped. I apologized.

And Francis said, "It's all right Dominic, I understand. Let's take it again. Try it again. Go back to the original name. Don't worry about it."

I was slightly relieved.

"Oh, but change the name of the other lawyer," Francis added, "Instead of Johnson, make it Jackson, okay?"

We did it again, and I went up on the line again. And Al was looking at me. And I was starting to get a little nervous.

"Take it again, Dominic."

Third time's the charm? Not really: Al got up and walked away. And I thought, "Well this must be the end of my movie career, I'm really screwing up here." Then Al came back in, sat down, and looked at me.

"Al, I'm sorry I screwed up," I sincerely pleaded, hoping to salvage my diminishing stake in the film business.

"No, Dominic. It's not you. It's not you," he assured.

"What do you mean?" And with a half-understanding of what Al was saying, we finally made it through the scene—which is exactly what Francis had been going for. Afterward, I realized what Francis had been doing. He had been manipulating me, making me nervous on purpose. And later on, when I saw the scene, I could see why.

On film, you have to know what you're saying—just say it authentically and the camera will pick up the nuances. If you are a good actor, it will all come out. You have to be real in front of the camera; you can't "act."

Francis had hired me because I looked right for the role of Johnny Ola: I had the right voice, the right attitude, and I knew how to act. But he also knew that I was a stage actor who had never really done film, so he purposefully manipulated me to get the performance he needed. By continually throwing me off balance, Francis coerced the catch in the throat out of me that Ola needed to deliver the speech. It made the apprehension in the scene real. It was a lesson I had to learn, and I remember saying to my inexperienced self at the time, "*I'll get even with you, Francis!*"

As we were doing the scene and I was talking to Al, the little boy entered wearing his white Communion suit. When I first saw him I had a flash of memory—much like the association Walt Witcover and Bernie Barrow had described—and I thought: he was *me* as a child, I could see it!

So when the little boy came over, I raised my eyebrow, just a millimeter, purposefully, to indicate something. And Francis said, "That's too much, Dominic."

"Oh, okay, Francis, you're right," I admitted. That's when I knew what film acting was.

That's when I realized that you don't do anything: you just believe what you are doing and say what you believe; you forget the camera's there. If a scene calls for a certain "largeness," you do it knowing there's no audience like in live theatre to feel or sense or intuit. You just understand your space, let the cinematographer handle the frame, and do what you've got to do.

And unfortunately for me, they wanted me to drive a car. The good: a car had four wheels so my own personal balance would not come into play, as had been *somewhat* of a minor factor when learning how to ride a bike mid-performance. The bad: New York City, great city that it is, offers all kinds of opportunity at every turn and for every whim—including the ability to realize that you are slowly meandering down the sidewalk faster than the adjacent stand-still traffic, and the light bulb going off above your head in acknowledgment of never needing or wanting to learn how to drive is appearing faster than a changed traffic light. Thus, in both my little understanding of relative vehicle motion and an attempt not to crack the thin ice I assumed my previous scene had put me on, I came up with two solutions: take it slow and swing it wide.

Automatic transmission: I survived the first round. I was able to successfully start the engine—I was on a roll. We were shooting the scene where I led Corleone to Hyman Roth's house and we were filming at Hialeah Race Track in Miami: no obstructions here, just nice and slow, nice and wide, and no one will know the difference, right? Well, except for maybe expert director Francis Ford Coppola.

"Dominic, you're coming around that curve awfully wide," Francis said.

No problem, I'll just overcorrect for the next take, and would a professional driver on set mind backing up the car to get it in place for the next take so I can, ahem, focus on my scene?

So we did another take, and this time, still going nice and slow, I made sure not to take it so wide—with all of the subtle adjustment of someone who has no idea what they're doing has—and I came around the corner, heading straight for a pole. And, needless to say, since the camera was attached to the front of the car, Francis declared, "Ohhhhhh!"

Of course, I again had to get the stunt driver to do my stunt work: putting a car in "reverse" and backing it up for the next take. And piecing this master deception together, Francis came over and joined me in the car, asking, "Why didn't you tell me you couldn't drive?"

In order to get work sometimes, an actor's desire to get the job is so strong that he or she may not lie outright on a resume, but if somebody asks such things as "Can you drive?" said actor, even if they can't, will say, "Sure!" Then, they pray they never have to deliver the goods. But I should have known, when talent of this caliber is involved, you always deliver the goods.

And Lee Strasberg, who played Hyman Roth, didn't let me forget it. We hung out together all throughout the shoot because we were in a lot of scenes together—Johnny Ola being Roth's henchman—and I came to discover that Lee was a very focused, very tough and firm artist. He even upset Pam once by commenting on Alex's rambunctiousness—he could be a particularly *social* toddler—telling her that Alex was "trainable."

But even though Lee could be unapologetically direct in his grandfatherly ways, I did learn an important lesson from him in our time together. We were at a *Godfather* party with Coppola and everybody while we were shooting in Santa Domingo, and Francis's father approached me and said, "Dominic, why don't you sing 'Chitarra Romana'?" I was so full of food and didn't really want to get up but I recognized the cultural significance of the request, so I convinced myself that I was doing everyone a favor and I got up and sang it—albeit stuffed and half-heartedly. And afterward, Lee came over to me and said, "You know, you could have done that better." And though I was a little peeved by his criticism at the time, I also knew that what he was saying was right: if you're going to perform, then *perform*—or else don't do it.

Also determined to be right while we were in the Dominican Republic was: the Dominican Republic Army. The filming was wrapping up and had gone over a few weeks past scheduled—as is, not highly a big deal and can often be the case. This, however, was slightly more problematic for Pam and me personally, as we had planned on Pam giving birth once back in New York, and now—still on location—the baby was due any day.

In one of our last nights there, Pam and I made a late-night talk show appearance with the Johnny Carson of the Dominican Republic. And the talk show host asked her in front of the national audience, "How do you feel about your baby being born in the Dominican Republic?"

And Pam, not ever having needed to rehearse the *finesse* of talk show appearances, and obviously having much bigger things on her mind regardless, honestly blurted: "As long as the baby's healthy, I don't care where it's born!"

Myself, being a little more accustomed to the idea of good PR, I decided I would now have to go overboard to compensate for this could-be perceived lack of tact. So I jumped in with, "Oh, I'm so happy! The Dominican people are beautiful." Looking to slay the beast before it awoke, I added the kill stroke: "I love the people—we've even named our little girl Dominica."

Dominica Chianese was born February 8 at the Clinica Abreu—unexpectedly in the Dominican Republic. She was such a cute little girl; we didn't have a basket to put her in so we placed her in a little drawer and presented her at the ambassador's house.

It was touching and almost surreal for Dominica to have been born outside of New York, so it was with even greater alarm when we were all getting on the plane to finally head back to the United States and six armed soldiers came running up, rifles brandished, halting the flight and yelling "Dominicana, Dominicana!" They wouldn't let me bring the baby home!

And in the midst of this instantly excited commotion— and always one for the sudden promise of opportunistic exploration—Alex decided to capitalize on the "grown-up problems" and quietly excused himself from the group, curious as to what the Dominican Republic airport *really* had to offer. Fortunately, security was as diligent about lost children as they were citizenship, and they quickly traced Alex's steps down a luggage chute.

Once Alex was kindly removed from running around the luggage carousel and investigating suitcases, we were all ushered into a reunion, mid armed escort. A nice young woman who was the liaison officer at the airport seemed to make sense of the whole thing and took me aside, saying, "Dominic, we'll settle this. But you may have to stay overnight."

So everyone else from the film shoot went back to New York, and I was huddled into a small room with two very little children and a hysterical wife, and the authorities insisting that our new baby was a Dominicana. Apparently, they'd gotten the notion after my *ultra-suave* overcompensation of a PR recovery on the national talk show—the killing stroke indeed effective, the sole result: a self-infliction.

Pam and I stayed up all night worrying, and the next morning entire nations' livelihoods were settled with the matter of a few dollars. Dominica was naturalized as a Dominican citizen and the group of soldiers stood around the jefe's office while they held her tiny pinky and put her fingerprint in their little red book. It was very sweet, actually. So Dominica had dual citizenship.

Once finally back in New York, we found that—despite our whisked-away existence into Hollywood lavishness: the stars, the parties, the locales—reality's daily grind had not budged an inch and in fact had been preparing for us the whole time. We were a family with a toddler and now a newborn too, and we were almost completely broke.

While *The Godfather: Part II* had been a big breakthrough in my career, the roles didn't pour in afterward and I had been paid a very low sum. Being a still unestablished screen actor, my salary had basically amounted to a short-lived, burned-through sustenance between the two families I couldn't support, and I quickly found myself unable to come up with a single subway token needed to get to an audition.

But I had to get to that audition. I'd been proven right in my ability by being sought out for *The Godfather*, and I knew that if I could just press a little further, the promise of a better life was within *my* means. So I walked into the 72nd Street subway station, took a look around, and jumped the turnstile.

And sure enough, a cop materialized out of nowhere and said, "Where're you going?"

I rapidly stiffened and froze; his question was instantly piercing—not just because I had gotten caught trying to sneak on the subway, but because in that policeman's most honest and necessary inquiry, I really didn't have an answer. I was a forty-three-year-old man, the father of two babies immediate and several children in waiting, trying desperately to get any kind of job, driven by merciful, temporary glimpses of "making it," and when reality's clouds of hope were disrupted and dissipated—as with this cop's question—I was left standing with the fact that, right now, in the only real place I lived, I couldn't even afford to get on the train.

However, things had been working behind the scenes in my favor. I, too, had a godfather.

Al Pacino and I had really bonded while working together on *The Godfather: Part II*. Al was a fellow New Yorker who also had trouble with his own driving during the shoot—"besting me," however, with his ability to do his own reverse, *albeit crookedly*—and we became much more than colleagues in our time together.

On my behalf, Al had recommended and then introduced me to esteemed director Sidney Lumet, who took one look at me and said, "Yep, you could be Sonny's father." And just like that, I was cast in *Dog Day Afternoon*—all because a friend had been watching out for me.

I only had one line in the film—"Why rob a bank when you got a sucker for a mother?"—but inadvertently thanks to Alex, I realized exactly how I was going to say it.

On the day of the shoot, Alex, picking up where his previous suitcase investigation down in Santa Domingo had left off, decided to resume operations with an acute focus to my alarm clock. This much was readily clear upon receiving a late phone call from a frantic AD, stating, "Um…Mr. Chianese? You're supposed to be here in Brooklyn!"

When I jumped out of the taxi half-dressed, I found Sidney sitting by a car, casually enjoying a sandwich and a coffee. He offered, "Well, Dominic, I bet you really must have been frightened when they woke you up this morning, right?"

"I'm sorry, Mr. Lumet. I'm so sorry I'm late"—this was not how I had envisioned my acting lifeline as going.

"That's okay, don't worry about it," Sidney calmly suggested. So we started chatting and I got a coffee as well; and it was through our unexpected and organic conversation that I decided that even though I only had one line, *I was going to act my heart out for this guy.* And I figured out how I was going to say the line—by using the image of my own father. And when I went to perform and say the line, it came out great—all initiated because of Alex being Alex.

I was very thankful for these sparse acting jobs when they came along; but thankful was one sentiment and coming close to eviction was another. It came down to doing whatever I could just to stay afloat.

Somebody recommended me for a job as the private secretary to the head of NASA—seriously—and I had no choice but to take it. After graciously accepting the position, the acceptance consisting mostly of sheer restraint at the joy of possibly making rent, I soon learned just why this position had remained available.

Robert Jastrow, the head of the NASA program, had a well-deserved reputation as "hard to work for" and usually outlasted his secretaries by a ratio of: infinity to one month. The guy was incredible. He once made it a point to make me aware and understanding—while he was driving—of how many seconds there are in a week. He was working on a project one time and he cut his hand with an X-Acto knife. I mean, he cut it bad: he was bleeding all over. But instead of going to the hospital like any sensible person with knowledge of the body's finite amount of fluid, he just wrapped it up and kept going. This *was* NASA after all, and he was going to personally make sure that worlds were sought and conquered.

I was supposed to be helping him put a book together or something when a woman who worked in the office—who must have crunched the secretary-to-Jastrow numbers and realized that I had already outlived the formula's quotient—said with honest wonderment, "Oh, you work for Jastrow. I don't know how you can handle him; he's a tough cookie."

And I replied with equal earnestness, "Yeah, but I really want to be an actor. Or a singer."

Then, she proffered something that I had truly not fully considered in its entirety up until that very point: "You know, you can do 'em both."

Why not? My coworker at NASA was right. Do it all: be an actor *and* a singer. Follow your dream. I had always considered the two arts to be on separate paths—that inevitably, one had to be chosen over the other. And this duality had been limiting in its desired expectation. I was in a dead-end job, from what I could tell, and was thinking that the way forward had to be a certain way. Her advice was almost unbinding: whatever my soul would urge me toward was whatever I should probably do.

So it was really more an aftermath when Jastrow eventually fired me out of his own obsessiveness. I was warmly thanked by an understanding NASA commission for my own uncharted explorations: I'd held out as private secretary for almost half a year.

Emancipated and enlivened, I completely opened myself to whatever and however life's journey would bring. But I couldn't help but realize that the same soul that was my uninhibited guide was severely lacking where I needed it most: in my very home.

Because while I had basically resolved to living off of short-term jobs that enabled survival on the fringes of poverty,

Pam, most assuredly, had not. The evidence of which was so clearly laid out at our growing and empty address.

On the surface, it was fairly easy to see why Pam seemed to be going through a postpartum phase ever since we had gotten back to New York: we barely had any money, despite my film appearances; my "survival" jobs hardly lasted long enough to be counted as "temporary"; my acting career, though now involving said film, was stalling at a certain level; and she was taking care of two young children with scarcity—which was a long way from the professional dancer that she had originally gone to New York to become.

But there was more. Pam would say, "We don't have enough fun together." And she was right. That was extensively where our relationship remained. We never really had a deeper understanding. We kind of existed together to the backdrop of something else always going on. Whether it was the play in Boston, or my movie roles, or the jobs I'd work in between, there was always this drive, this "agenda" that stood in our way. Neither one of us really questioned it: we just rode the rails like the train we came in on, where we had initially met.

But still, there was more. Even if I removed the pretentions, there were things there that I didn't want to admit. She would have friends over to the house, and they would take sides on issues or topics that would occur between Pam and I in conversation; they would act very divisive. And aside from her "friend" Casey, she had mostly women over to visit—definitely not a problem and possibly more "acceptable" in itself—but many of these women were rough. They dressed and acted extremely tough: I had an idea of what was going on.

And since I didn't want to acknowledge what I was fairly certain was happening, I bottled up all of this tension; I carried around my expanding fears and stress. At forty-three years old, I started having anxiety attacks.

The first one happened while I was holding Dominica. I was in our apartment, cradling her in my arms, and walking her to sleep. And—since I was now going with any endeavor or urge that came my way—I was also creating a song in my head at the same time. The song was about living in New York, and I had a thought suddenly occur where I remembered a friend of mine from Los Angeles had invited me to move out there, where my film career might be expedited. I realized that this could be true, but then I thought about how my heart and my children from my first marriage were all in New York; and I guess it was just too much to work through with all of my ongoing stress and turmoil, so I just lost it. The guy who lived upstairs had to come down and take Dominica while they put me in the ambulance.

The second one came while filming on location. I was playing one of the men involved with the Watergate break-in, in the film *All the President's Men*, and we had just finished shooting all but one of my scenes down in Washington, DC. My time away from home allowed me the unfortunate opportunity to see that my marriage was really in more trouble than I had thought, and I desperately reached for anything to calm me down: I partook in the mid-'70s, I took a toke. But I probably should have known that even in this self-medicating "remedy" I would go against the grain.

Whereas most people zoned out, I honed in on my inner perception of compounding problems. I broke down inwards; I projected it outwards: people could see that something was wrong. The wonderful actor F. Murray Abraham, who was also in the film, said, "We've got to get him to a hospital." Even in my condition, I was so appreciative—he really helped me out and conveyed he understood.

The insightful old German doctor at the hospital attempted to shed light on it. He asked, "How did you learn acting?"

"I taught myself," I plainly replied.

He accepted this and responded, "Well, I'm going to give you a Valium. I know you don't like to take it, but you're going to need it." From his one single question, he had correctly and revealingly surmised that I tried to solve my own problems without any outside help.

Upon returning, I emotionally skipped past what I *undoubtedly* knew was taking place within my home life and immediately fell into the "high life" scene. There was a known hostess, Tula, a very cultured, modernized, and intellectual woman herself, who had an open salon where artists and all kinds of interesting people would converge. Wonderful musicians would come and play there often, and conversations would easily drift toward all things theatre. And since I wasn't getting the loving and nurturing that I thought I needed from Pam, the need to just be held that I couldn't convey, I convinced myself that I, too, "deserved" the extramarital activity that abounded in the culture, that it was okay to pursue Tula.

Tula also got me a job as an administrator with an organization that catered to young people suffering from schizophrenia—just when I needed it least. Some of these people were very clinically sick—one patient even got hostile—and while I was grateful to still be surviving to the next month's bill cycle, I would come home completely exhausted and depressed.

My dwindling saving grace was a singing gig I managed to secure at O'Lunney's a couple of nights a week—and I was still occasionally performing at Folk City—but none of these "quick fixes" were going to last by any means: my solution was more. I met another woman at Tula's salon, Russi. I became involved with her too. Then there was Louise. And as long as I kept my head in the clouds, I didn't have to face having never *really* known Pam—*powerlessly* sitting atop while watching my second family fall apart.

So it was with one of survival's most desperate limps that I entered New Year's Eve 1975, receiving a phone call from a friend who had no idea what he was requesting to join.

"Dominic, do you mind if I just sit in with you, just to play harmonica a little bit?"

"All right," I muttered. Anything you want, I thought— let's just get this year over with.

And while we were playing this commemorative set—
to which my commemorative spirit lay solely in song—the
music became a captor, channeled expression became my
freedom. I started to loosen up a little and thought: all in all,
things could be worse. Then Louis, Folk City's doorkeeper,
came over to confirm what I had figured was the real truth
all along: they were.

"Dominic, there's four policemen out there. They want
to see you."

"Wait'll I finish," I laid out. I decided I deserved at least
one last solace. And the cops must have had their New Year's
spirit too, because they actually obliged. So we finished out the
performance, I walked off stage, and the police arrested me.

"What for?" It was the honest truth.

"Well, you deserted your children," one of the officers
observed plainspoken. Merle had told the police that I
"deserted" them because I hadn't gone to family court that
week. She had doubled down on her persistence, acting upon
the notion that I was secretly loaded from the film appearances she had heard I was doing. And since it was Saturday
night on New Year's Eve, all the courts were closed—so in the
system I went.

But before they locked me away and threw out the key,
I got my one phone call. I told Pam I wouldn't be home for
New Year's.

"All right," Pam easily stated. "We'll have the party
anyway." Her dismissive acceptance struck me as odd, especially knowing that while I was here, Casey was there; but

the thought was nonetheless rendered indifferent: my time was up.

The next morning, it was a new year: the rise of promise, the dawn of something new—I was heading out to Rikers Island. Thrown in the paddy wagon with all of the other hardened criminals, I decided my "crime" wouldn't stack up well with such things as "murder" and that it was best to keep quiet for the one-way ride up north.

The holding pen, however, did not allow for such evasiveness. Free to roam about in our thug-packed facility, my block mates started to sniff me out.

"Hey, Pop, what are you in for?" I was forty-four but unshaven and unkempt, so I must have looked twenty years older—I surely did not want to answer.

"Hey, whadda you in for?" Now, everybody in the cell got quiet and turned their attention my way. I knew I couldn't hold out; I stood out too much—I was the only Caucasian in there. Thirty guys crowded me and waited for the response.

"C'mon, whaddya in for?!"

I was getting scared now. I just went with the truth. I just went with two words:

"A woman."

And the place erupted.

I was in. I was *in*.

"Man, I hope you beat the hell out of her," some guy shared with me.

Then everything calmed down and we started passing around cigarettes. And as tensions gave way to cigarette smoke, another guy came over and we had a Rikers heart-to-heart: "You never been in jail before, right? I could tell," he explained; then he added, "You know, they told me I murdered this guy, but I didn't murder him."

I spent the rest of New Year's Day 1976 in there, and it ended up being a good experience in a lot of ways: I was able to use it in my acting.

Six months later, Merle had me arrested again. They didn't send me back with the "boys," but I did receive a stern warning: I had to send some money. But the truth was that I was month-to-month at best, and Merle didn't get it. She had this idea that any screen time equated an instant fortune, and she was *attacking* like a bee that had just stumbled upon limitless nectar: she just kept coming.

Eventually, I had to explain why litigation held our "family" together. I told Dominic Jr., who was eleven at the time, "You know, your mother put me in jail." And he rejoiced, "Don't worry, Pop, it's only chicken wire!" But whereas he could make light of it, I could not. By then, I considered any and all emotional attachment to Merle done.

And Pam and I were not much better. We had not really been together as man and wife for over a year. We lived in the same house and "mutually" raised our children, but there was no conversation, no romance, or any pending thought thereof. Our constant lack of money and *exclusive* lifestyles were starting to take their tolls.

I thankfully managed to get an acting job at the Goodman Theatre in Chicago, but it was almost secondary to my insurmountable stress. I was cast in Israel Horovitz's *Our Father's Failing* trilogy, and the irony of the title was nowhere near lost on me. Pam brought Alex and Dominica out to Chicago, but our time there only confirmed what we already knew.

When they left, I had an affair that resulted in an anxiety attack: a depletion intensified, the icing on *my* cake. I was so distraught and paranoid over everything that I ended up accusing the *girl* as a user because I suspected she was "cheating" on me by flirting with the paramedic.

I was in a bad place and I came home to a worse one. Even with the acting work, we couldn't make rent. I had to ask for an extension, and the marshals were set to come and evict us. And though I managed to scrape it together and stave off eviction, Pam just couldn't handle it anymore. She was an only child from Ohio who grew up very middle class in a nice, spacious house: she couldn't deal with eking out a growing family in a working-class walk-up.

She warned me she was going to leave; I truly begged her not to go. We might have been embarking on different lifestyles; we might have already drifted apart; but I pleaded with her not to break up our family, that we could figure out something, anything for the sake of our children.

Then, hearing all of this, and in a final desperation, Pam picked up the phone and called her parents. And on May 19, 1976, Pam got into their car with our two children, and they left.

And I remembered a time, from the beginning of our relationship, when Pam had been on the phone with her ex-boyfriend, and how she had dismissed him kind of coldly. Not angrily, but coldly. And my intuition then was that she was going to hurt me.

And she did.

Chapter 8

TZIPPY

"Oh, God."

Al Pacino had said it best.

"You mean Pam left with the kids? She just left?"

"Yeah."

We were sitting in Joe Allen's restaurant and I could see how much he understood the kind of pain I was in, what compassion he really had. It was very dark and I needed a friend to help pick me up, and Al was a very dear friend.

When Pam got to Ohio, she immediately filed for divorce: she was intent on marrying Casey. I kept calling, hoping to at least hear the voices of our children—accepting the divorce as the cost to once more knowing our children's laugh. But Pam had our children's surnames changed to Casey's semi-unpronounceable Polish name, and there was no way left to reach them.

I wasn't the only one in our vacated apartment—the grounds were now haunted with thoughts: how it had come to this, how it had ceased to be, how it never really was. I painfully probed to the beginning, and saw our lack of warmth. Pam and I were never truly honest with each other: we hadn't taken the time to *know*. I had suspected things that turned out to be true, which had kept me away and had driven her elsewhere. Lack of money had been the excuse, but our love wasn't built to stand up and last.

It all began to remind me of how I had picked the wrong partner, how I had been the wrong partner for her. I quit my position with the psychiatric organization—it was from a *different time*. I eventually had the apartment boxed, and the man who lived next door cried when I told the storage company to "just take everything."

I didn't know where to go; the bottom of my life had just fallen out: Rebecca, Dominic Jr., and Sarah were just over the Brooklyn Bridge—an unreachable Alex and Dominica were now hundreds of miles away.

Maybe there was hope I might somehow reach them if I stayed on the periphery of their lives. I thought back to and contacted a mutual friend that Pam and I knew, Cathy Bacon, who was a dancer at the Rehearsal Club—of which Pam had originally sought. She and her friend Rene Roy were benevolently welcoming. Soothing and assuring, Cathy said, "Dominic, you can stay at my apartment. When I go to work, you'll have the place to yourself."

At first it was day to day, and it was very hard to be alive. Cathy would come home and hear me crying, and I became extremely dependent. She and Rene would take good care of me and encourage me to get out when I was able to pull it together for a few hours, accompanying me to the movies, knowing my fondness of film. And on July 4, 1976, when we all celebrated the country's bicentennial at the apartment and watched the tall ships go by, that intuitive spark that was somewhere in there, that always persisted and ever remained, saw a sense of direction in this nation's spirit, and opened itself to glimmer more.

An electric guitar and a gig at Garr's restaurant: I had to keep things going. And while I didn't necessarily flock first toward the electric style, I knew I couldn't stay miserable indefinitely; plus, it always brought energy and made people dance. My mother's cousin was the bartender; my first cousin Jerry and his friends from Wall Street would come down and say, "Someday you're going to make it"; and if I could bring myself to hold my head up long enough, I could look out and see Cathy and Rene on the dance floor too. The small world expanded to include familiar faces, and they began to remind me of who I once was.

I poured myself into my acting, my music taking care of itself. *All the President's Men* was released later that year, and I did an episode of *Kojak* as well. Al Pacino personally arranged for me to be brought into a project with him at the members-only Actors Studio. And Raul Julia stood beside me as I broke down and declared "*Miseria!*" outside of his apartment. Thus, the theatre family readied what I needed most: a steadiness through my hurtful terrain.

And just as sure footing trusted its guide, a glowing light was taken too soon. My sister Frances could barely talk: a cancerous disintegration of body and brain. She was forty-three years old with a family of four, and only a few words left. With nothing to offer but deterioration's observance, my family's words were fewer.

There was no history of what was happening, of this type of sickness; and her untimely departure was unprecedented in our lineage. And because Frances and my father were always so close, it was in her passing when I saw it first: that a steadfast support was no longer impenetrable, that impossible stability had run its source dry. Having never before succumbed to adversarial condition, my sister's death was where my father fell hard.

Music was the healing: it was my forgetfulness; it was my passion. If I could pick up my guitar, if I could sound out the entire tune, then I'd have no choice but to relinquish my troubles, at least for a little while.

So it was at O'Lunney's in 1977 when I was drowning myself in song and verse, existing for just one more opportunity to perform and pretend I only existed on stage, when I ran headfirst into the French.

We were introduced.

"You have an accent...are you French?" the cultured world traveler in me asked.

"No, I'm Israeli," Zipporah reported.

It was somewhere over coffee later that night and the Israeli Day Parade—which just happened to be the next morning—where I decided that I could not bear to let Tzippy, as I so affectionately called her, get anywhere out of my sight.

"I haven't a night off, Domy," Tzippy teased after I saw her literally every night. And because I had now shielded the longing hurt with instant bliss through this sexy, voluptuous Israeli woman, I took "no nights off" to mean "still free mornings" and moved into her place on Lexington and 52nd.

Tzippy was a wonderful person and the epitome of a stable young woman. She had served in the Israeli Army at seventeen years of age and now worked for the Israeli consulate. She would educate me about survival and teach me Hebrew words such as *ein brera*, which meant: "You have no choice."

I quickly became very dependent on her despite knowing that our time was limited, that she had to return to Israel by the end of the year. But until that foreseen end with her, I wanted to relish every minute. So we both let go in our fated interim; we both slipped easily and gave it a name. We were quickly sickened not from expiration, but from what we understood and knew that we had.

We hopped on a plane and celebrated Tzippy's thirtieth birthday in Las Vegas. Then I got a residual check from *The Godfather: Part II* and we went straight to Rio.

It was ten days of beautiful paradise in Rio de Janeiro: the first time I had been out of the country purely for pleasure, the first time in a long time I remembered what pleasure was.

It was good to finally take things as is again, but even in this I saw cracks in the armor.

I had been expecting another residual check to arrive and reimburse our international adventure, but it never did, so I was essentially spending up most of my money. And while this caused me to get very anxious, there was a greater underlying tension that this improbable utopia, not just our tropical leisure but the improbable utopia of Tzippy and myself, had a dated shelf life and was coming to a close.

And maybe Tzippy realized this too, because just before we left, she taught me a final important lesson about survival. We were hiking through the rainforest outside of Rio and came upon an anthill on the forest floor. Tzippy grabbed a twig and placed it in front of the anthill, blocking the line of ants maneuvering to and fro. Then she said, "Watch." And the ants just slowly walked around the obstacle—determined to keep going, they made another way. In her understanding of how the world worked, Tzippy had taught me about overcoming. She had shown me how I could move on.

Our trip, our relationship, and Tzippy's warm presence all came to a close at once. I tried to fight the instant devastation, pulling out every last effort I had. It was more than just Tzippy returning home; it was the tatters of what I now sadly called mine.

"I'll become a Jew for you; I'll come to Israel," I desperately reasoned with little understanding. Anything, I thought, to perpetuate *us*, to keep me from looking within.

"My folks would never accept you," Tzippy kindly dismissed with a truly empathetic small laugh.

Even if I were an expert driver, I'm not sure I could have handled it that day. Tzippy's friend drove us all to the airport; I cried most of the time. And as we pulled away, and the distance increased, Tzippy slowly faded out of my life. An impression burned brightly, she had strengthened my being, and reminded me that there was light.

I poured over the memories; I recycled the hope; I clung to everything learned. In my storming anguish, Tzippy's words stood unmoved: she had wanted to make sure I'd seen. *Ani ohev otach meod* could undo anything; she taught me to know: "I love you very much."

And Kenny had a love too. Kenny, or "Ken" when we were inebriated and getting short, loved the blues. And he had an equal infatuation for drinks. And fortunately for this Southern former pugilist, Kenny hadn't taken enough hits to indefinitely blunt his small playwriting "career"—of which he so eagerly wanted me to star in. It all sounded pretty good, at least from where I sat—on the receiving end at O'Lunney's for once—and as long as Ken was buying, all I had to do was nod "yes" while I delved deeper into escape; misery closing in, always hot on the trail. And this went on for two days.

Emerging from this boozy stupor of "sure thing Ken" and "pick a family, any family" that I had forsaken, ruined the chances of, or dangled out in front, I had the great notion that everything was "fine" and that "I should live alone"— having found at least one way to cope. And apparently I had done all of the right nods, because Kenny—as was proper to fully name out in such times of clarity—had secured me a gig to introduce blues singers down in the Village.

But B.B. King had other plans. When I went to do this one-night-only job, I told Mr. King that I would be introducing him.

And he said, "No, no, I'll introduce myself." The King of the Blues rightfully issued his decree: he couldn't chance a cat diminishing his cool. Still, I had done a good job with the other guys, and it was like what Billy Joel was singing at the time: you have a drink, people applaud, and you think, "Well, I'm back in show business!"

I went with the obvious, of the "close to sure thing"—I resumed my Italian connection. The wonderful playwright Mario Fratti was doing a stage version of Fellini's *8½* at the Actors Studio and was looking to fill the central role of Italian-speaking, song-carrying, woman-obsessing Guido Contini. Mario thought I would be great for the part. I'd known him since working together in the '60s; from his surmising, he must have known me longer.

Barely holding it all together, I was getting by on the skin of my teeth—literally. One scene in *8½* called for me to be under the covers in skimpy underwear with a beautiful blonde; I figured I could somehow handle it. But since everything in my life but my actual acting was in such confused disarray, in one particular rehearsal, I showed up so late that I skipped wardrobe altogether and simply hopped in the bed. And at some point in the scene, the actress went to pull off the covers, and there I was, stark naked at the Actors Studio. Everybody applauded and Billy Joel was right: I was back in the flesh indeed.

More Actors Studio projects came my way, and I was graciously able to avoid myself. *Our Father's Failing* was being put on at the Studio, and since I had the specific experience, I was given the opportunity to perform it with one of America's greatest actors, Michael Moriarty.

Throughout the performance, Michael could see that I was really on edge and in a very fragile state. I got into a "disagreement" with one of the other actresses who wanted me to do something outlandish with the gun prop, and Michael quickly intervened. Michael knew I was right—not to get too fantastical with the performance—but he could also see that my overly adverse reaction stemmed from something more.

Genuinely concerned for another artist, Michael suggested I might go see Holly Hein, a psychotherapist he knew who worked with a variety of people in show business. So I went over to Holly's office on West 72nd Street and I took my shoes off, and we began talking; and for some reason, the little violin that my father made me put away suddenly sprang into my mind.

Synthesizing all of this, Holly stated, "You may have issues." Then she assured, "All you really need is work, Dominic." And since being flighty had served me *so* well, I took it to mean "acting work" and assumed that all I had to do was stay employed.

Unfortunately, the engagements at the Actors Studio were all limited run, and I soon found myself at my new apartment in Tudor City, sitting alone with an avocado plant.

But for a short while I even made this work, using the guitar I kept with me as therapy. Then, the song ended and I put the guitar down. I could see that I'd lost it all.

I got it in my head: "I'm going to be sexy now"—I was going to climb those stairs. Someone had told me about the place on Lexington where I might be able to buy my way out. Just give the guy at the top step your money and dignity, and then you would have it all. And I would always pick a new one, because there were always new girls; I gave myself better odds to find *love*. It was justified because it was the intimacy I was after, I would replay to myself while getting crushingly stoned.

And under the best desperate circumstances I could shed my guilt and trade it for looming depression. My diminution became my cause: the less I existed, the less I hurt.

But I couldn't keep up with the glory I lived for, those moments when there was nothing else. I had to surpass them or else I'd reflect, and be forced to live out the damage incurred.

So I started going to *those* clubs in the '70s where everyone sat around nude. I felt dirty and ashamed and didn't know what to do, and the whole time I would be lit. I even tried my luck in Atlantic City, but I couldn't outrun myself.

In this spiraling state of exploitation, something told me to reach out to the *user* I met in Chicago. And she agreed to come visit, proving to be anything *but*, because those few days never brought us *together*. We conversed and shared, and I prospected for hope, briefly sifting the pain and revealing connection.

Sufficiently revitalized with just enough confidence, I was cast as and commanded a leading role in David Mamet's *The Water Engine*. We were well reviewed in *The New York Times* and other publications, the show garnering the momentum for a Broadway run. Renowned acting teacher Charlie Laughton, seeing the performance, asked how I was able to play Mr. Wallace the candy store owner so exact, saying, "It felt like you were back in the 1930s. How did you do that?"

There would occasionally come a time when the pounding past I carried—in this case the candy store from the Bronx—would manifest itself through burning, furious passion and produce moments in my course that I could rest upon as *useful*. It was in my acting where I exclusively found these; it was in these moments I lived for.

Repose did not loosen obligation, however, and I was still a father on both sides of the stage. Splitting had come at my children's expense—single-parenting no match for the calling streets of Brooklyn.

I knew Dominic Jr. was already into *things*, disbelief sparing the full report, and I thought I could keep a particularly watchful eye if I could divert his attention to the role of Bernie, the young teenage boy at the candy store in *The Water Engine*.

Acclaimed director Joe Papp agreed and said to bring Dominic Jr. in. But I couldn't get Dominic Jr.'s mother to consent: Merle had seen the life of a thespian firsthand. She said, "No. I don't want him to be an actor. I don't want him to do this."

And Joe, now personally invested in the matter, heard about Merle and said, "Oh really?" Then, he phoned Merle like an overseeing uncle and appealed to her on a mutually Jewish level, saying, "Listen, you're Jewish, the kid is Jewish. This is a tradition." I couldn't believe how he had talked to Merle!—I could never get away with talking like that. Of course, it easily worked: Dominic Jr. was instantly hired, but never actually went on.

It was troubling to be let down in my fatherhood, that I couldn't pull enough strings and actually get him on stage. I had hoped to intervene and possibly change his life's direction, to get him away from where I knew he was going. And as sad as it was, *this* was the extent of my ability. Performance is where I had hoped to bring him to; life is where he needed me most. But outside of the theatre, I was drowning my sorrows. In this I was succeeding: like father, like son.

I had a temporary office job to make ends meet, I had my role in *The Water Engine* to avoid wit's end, and I had Ken— and it was definitely "Ken" at this point—to guide me as I plunged. And the ex-prizefighter in Ken was raring to go.

So when four pretty Irish sisters walked into O'Lunney's toward the end of 1977 and asked me if I could do them a favor, Ken found my Heineken-induced acceptance a little too indifferent, leaned in with his wouldn't-make-weight stature, and authoritatively declared with the inflection that whatever plan made was now definitely happening, "Hey, what's goin' on?"

One of the sisters explained the brilliant quagmire: "These people at the bar up the street, they have a picture that belongs to me on their wall. Could you help me get it? The bartender won't give it to me."

Though I was still mourning Tzippy and the fact that a wonderful relationship had immediately ended without my personal undoing, I still possessed enough foresight—at least at this point into the Heinekens—to realize that something was up. But reservation was hardly given a breath's deliberation because Ken had stepped in the ring:

"Yeah, don't worry, *we'll* come and get it for you." And it wasn't so much that Ken seemed to mean every word and, having finally found purpose, was in one of his "less challenge-able" moods, nor was it one too many suds talking—because it never usually was; no, it was simply the fact that I just couldn't stand it anymore and welcomed all things sweet release. So I banded up with these makeshift renegades and paraded to the bar up the street. I flipped my collar up because it was cold out; I unwisely tried to come off colder.

We walked into the bar and the whole thing played out more ridiculous than it sounded:

"You guys took my picture," one of the Irish sisters demanded, as if her life would change upon retrieval.

"Is that the picture?" sharp-as-a-tack Ken investigated, pointing to the picture on the wall. Acknowledging that there was in fact a picture on the wall, the Irish sister nodded "yes."

"Well, then git it," Ken emphasized to the bartender with his flaring Southern charm. And during this cunning exchange, as I was standing straight and stiff behind them, silent and collar up, acting like an enforcer modeled on George Raft or some other movie gangster, I had a moment of self-reflection, a touching introspective epiphany: "*What the hell am I doing here?*"

But the bartender, wise enough to quickly bow out of this mess, handed me the picture before I could think it through. I, too, still possessing reasoning in the lower gears, decided I also wanted out and swiftly scooped up the portrait and headed for the door. However, just before I could make a clean break, the Irish sister reaffirmed our menace, further committing me to my role: "You know what these guys would have done to you if you didn't give them the picture?"

The next day, *The Water Engine* was reviewed in *The New York Post*, and I was surprised to find out who read such reviews: the Irish mafia. The *Post* had run my picture alongside the play's review, and these really tough-looking Irish guys "representing" the bar we had been in the night before—and I had been around enough to know who they most likely were—came bursting into O'Lunney's, shouting, "There he is!"

They swarmed around me, and one of the guys collectively spoke with an astuteness that would have made Ken proud: "Did you take that thing?"

"Yeah."

"Why?"

"Because I thought it was the girl's," I carefully submitted.

And while it seemed that the details of the matter might have been uncovered at a snail's pace by this method, someone on the O'Lunney's staff must have sensed that these guys were about to cut to the *real-quick*, and since Ken had the morning off—from drinking—because of his big night, they took it upon themselves to thankfully defend and intervene: "Dominic just had one too many drinks the other night. He's really a nice guy."

That held them off for about two weeks. The next time, it was two detectives who came in, looking to question me about a robbery. Harry, the bartender at O'Lunney's, gave me the heads-up: "Run downstairs and go hide with the Chinese cook. We'll put you in the dumbwaiter."

When I eventually *resurfaced*, I found that everything was still waiting for me—albeit now with the added responsibility of having to go see a lawyer. He wanted to know who the "other guy" was, but Kenny—as I knew him formally—was a "buddy" at best who was gone. I chillingly learned that the portrait was just a game piece in a bar feud gotten way out of hand. The situation itself had a familiar ring: it was ever indicative of me.

I was forty-six years old and hiding out in bars' kitchens, living scantily day to day. My judgment was corrupted by my burdensome pain; I only existed to step into roles. I had pushed away or lost so many I loved; thank goodness I made a new friend.

Joan Detz was a very bright redhead in her mid-twenties who I met through the temporary office work I was doing at the time. She had a little apartment in Brooklyn near Merle's, and I would drop by and see her after I would see my children. We decided we would just be friends.

She was a speechwriter for Brooklyn Union Gas, and I encouraged her to enter a writing contest, which she won. It was good to know I had *someone* when I returned from performances. And when we tried briefly to be more than "just friends," we could see it wouldn't last. We graciously reverted—we realized what we'd already had.

Rays of light were coming to find me; I hadn't made them all go away. In 1978, I received an offer to join the Eugene O'Neill Theater Center for summers in Waterford, Connecticut, where actors were given a script and asked to create something in four days. It was a selective grouping of actors with proven ability: I was back on the road to self-esteem. Amongst other wonderful actors and playwrights, I was surrounded in art and repurposed in life.

Suddenly, I was being *sought*; my talents were actually wanted. I had two movies released that year, *On the Yard* and *Fingers*, and I was filming two more: *And Justice for All* with Al Pacino and *Firepower* with Sophia Loren. And during our filming of *Firepower*, Sophia thankfully came to my rescue.

The director, Michael Winner, who had a reputation for yelling at underlings, was trying to get me to cram under a desk, which I couldn't do because the cameraman already had dibs. But before I could convey this complex aforementioned, Michael had already started in, making sure his reputation stood good. I could feel my blood rising but was trying to maintain, thinking this guy might actually fire me while filming in Curaçao—I could be stuck getting home!

Out of respect for Sophia and the potential long walk, I restrained and remained at "ease." And Sophia, with her observant and exemplary professionalism, must have seen what was taking place because she stoically leaned over and gracefully lessoned in my ear: "We can get through this."

And in the middle of this sudden bursting work, I even got an invitation for a full-time singing gig down in Atlantic City after the head of Resorts International heard me perform. They were going to give me the full ride: a nice hotel room and everything—I was heavily considering it. But the night before I was set to commit, I got a call from Curt Dempster, the artistic director of the Ensemble Studio Theatre, who said, "I'd like to invite you to be a member of EST."

Curt told me they were doing Vincent Canby's *End of the War*, directed by David Margulies, and they wanted me to be the captain. And since the EST was a respected developing ground for new plays, of course I jumped at the chance.

But I still had to deal with Atlantic City. They were expecting me, and even if I knew what kind of trouble I might get into down there—girls, games, *girls*—that had been my intention since I didn't have any other full-time job initially lined up. I picked up the phone and made the call; I gave them a weak excuse. And by the way the people in Atlantic City cryptically stated "*You owe us one*," somehow I knew they meant it.

I had played my cards right: Al Pacino soon after hired me for *Richard III*. I was Tyrrell and it was a good part—my mouth further watered for Shakespeare. We started out in Philadelphia and then moved to the Cort Theatre in New York, and it was here that I really got to know Al well.

Al had a softball team composed of his friends, and he would send a car to pick us up and take us all to play on the banks of the Hudson. We would laugh and play ball and afterward dine, and Al would then have the car take us home. If I ever ran into him at a restaurant, he would always invite me over to the table, never directing conversation to himself. His door was always open to any of his friends, no matter what the situation might be.

Al had a great personality; he was always uplifting to be around—his friendship made all the difference. One time, Al noticed a green velvety jacket I had bought at Bloomingdale's for sixty bucks and said, "Gee, that's a nice jacket. Can I borrow that for a minute?" The next thing I knew, he came in wearing it as Richard III. It was very funny, on the spot. Al was an enormous artist with an even bigger heart. I felt very fortunate to know him.

The show itself was also a huge success, led by a very powerful Richard in the audience-favorite Al. He had hired many of his friends to be a part of it, and it was after the performances where *I* would come alive, leading us in song with my guitar. And even though my character's presence was continually cut short, the joys of the comradeship relit what was inside and showed me that something was trying to regrow.

So when another summer of the O'Neill Playwrights Conference came up in 1979, I reluctantly asked Al if it was okay that I left. And, of course, Al said, "Yeah, it's all right. You can go. Go ahead, Dominic." But before I did, he threw me a going-away party at Café Un Deux Trois and we all had a great time. At one point, I stood up on a chair and sang "Guantanamera."

And while the song "Guantanamera" was about lamenting a girl that got away, I felt *I* had come far enough to move on. So when I met the taller Nordic blonde Ann Zeigler at the O'Neill Playwrights Conference that summer, I waited some, but not too much, before I went all in.

Ann was a teacher who was at the conference as part of an effort to learn more about education and creative arts. I was glad to see that the educational system was slowly coming around—even gladder to see that Ann was single. The old, familiar friend felt good, and it was something to the effect of, "Ann, I think I'd better hold on to you, I might slip," when I first seized my opportunity at her vulnerability.

I moved into her house in Connecticut, and since Ann had been previously married to a Greek, I met all of Ann's joyous Greek friends. She had a friend named Socrates who was a practicing psychotherapist, and he knew I had things going on.

It didn't last too long; we had different ideas on things—different ideas of how to control. Ann could be very demanding and liked to drink, *always* keeping a wine on hand. But in our time together, as brief as it was, Ann helped me cope with what I couldn't face: I had survived relationships that had come and gone, but was never prepared for my father dying.

Chapter 9

1981

was aimless.

As long as I was acting, I had direction—literally—but left to my own devices, I was a man enshrouded with guilt.

My children were getting older—Pam still wouldn't let me see them; I was forty-nine and bouncing between relationships that didn't work and my parents' place; and my ailing father had yet to see his son maintain. My acting roles were my window to life; I needed *A Time for Miracles*.

John Forsythe was the star of *A Time for Miracles*, a film about Mother Elizabeth Seton, the woman who established the first girls' Catholic school in the nation. I was cast as the priest who promoted Mother Seton's canonization, and the role of helping someone else's cause helped lift my own burden as well.

Kind and understanding, seasoned actor John Forsythe also aided in my temporary reprieve with his unfailing cordiality and rides in his personal limo. The acting community kept me from going astray: I was never permitted to wander too far.

There were all these people on Fifth Avenue, and I knew I was one of them, but somehow I really wasn't. They all appeared destined in their determined courses. They all seemed to know where they were going.

So many of them too, from all over the world, came down just to make an amends. Lost in the crowd, I felt shepherded in: a sheep on the steps with his thoughts. I sat outside the entrance of Saint Patrick's Cathedral, torn between the part of me already in.

I searched for the twenty-fourth pew because I was born on the twenty-fourth of February; I searched for a place to call *mine*. There was nowhere left to run, no behavior that could hide me; I was finally naked in shame.

Eleanor had deserved someone better; Lissa was the one who was true. I had walked out on my children and had them taken from me, and had knowingly used and been used.

I could see that I had been running to women, escalating to sex, in the hopes that intimacy *might* follow. My self-righteous solution had been repetitious: I sincerely believed I was seeking out love.

But had I not given my heart to at least some of these women? Or had I divorced my heart from my soul? I had children with Merle, and she had wanted them; but I could not relinquish my art. Pam had wanted children, and I did as well; but that didn't mean that I knew *how* to love.

I looked up from the pew, and there was a cross, and I prayed, "Dear God, please forgive."

My devotion to family was not as strong as I'd thought, but had it ever been enough to be *love?* I had been desperate; I had been needy; I had needed a clearer path. I had searched for vindication, for recognition as an artist, for proof my identity was real. I had fought for my families and lived for my passion, and in the end sided with one.

Nothing was ever planned except to somehow make it, and whatever would come came confused. I involved different women with wrongful emotions, then failed when I salvaged my *role*.

Who was I who thought *I could go get it all*, who lived only in those *other* days? So many who cared for me needed me now, but I was nowhere I knew to be found.

Then I looked ahead, I looked at the cross, and saw that it always remained. I wasn't quite sure what all of it meant, but I realized that I needed love.

I spoke how I knew that there was still good, that I knew God could still make a way. I gave up my capacity to carry the world; I accepted myself and cried.

And as I wept harder than I'd ever known, I could see I was nothing, alone.

So with tears in my eyes, I finally looked *up*, and knew that the cross remained.

I would never find what I thought I had sought: a tangible peace attained. There was no way to institutionalize it in any way, shape, or form. God was in you. And I was forgiven.

A strength swept over me; I knew I was loved; it was more than I ever had needed. I believed God had heard me in my darkest moment. I had made a connection. I really believed.

I had a new guidance; I wanted to give; I wanted to get it all back. I got my guitar out of hock because it was part of my soul; it was a way I could share it with others. And when I received the coupon returned, I tacked it to where I would remember. From the depths of despair to my bulletin board: the pawnshop had marked it *redeemed.*

So it was early '81 when I was riding the train home, sitting with my guitar and redemption. I was on the way back from working on David Mamet's *Lakeboat* in New Haven, minding my own business, when a girl noticed my freshly sprung instrument and said, "You're a musician. I know some musicians too."

"Oh." She couldn't see that I was in the middle of a life-changing epiphany.

"We have meetings down on 11th Street in the Village, if you want to come sometime," she opportunistically advanced.

"Well, maybe," I appeased, still having this other thing going on.

And when she left the train, I remembered that I *was* a changed man, that it was *okay* if I found her attractive. Transformations weren't all overnight: *so what if I picked up the phone?*

Janet was eager to meet, to show me her loft—to take me where all of them gathered. They were all very polite and very well dressed, but slightly too uppity for a chorus. And before I could process just where I had landed, Janet beseeched: "You must come to Carnegie Hall. They're going to give a concert with Mr. Mills—he's got white hair and elegance, and we all love him." So like cattle to the slaughterhouse, I followed her lead.

It was all very professional: everyone dressed the same; they were clearly well rehearsed in their song. And when these ten men and women performed their dissonant song-book of calculated gifts, they looked out into the audience but were miles away: their voices carrying for single approval, their eyesight burned at just one.

The evening's verses rang out for his glory—his hand-picked judgment of "good." Back in the real world, to the hundreds in the audience, everything came off *strange*. Being as much, it was with little surprise when Mr. Mills whispered: "Welcome to the group."

The cult conducted numerous rules with utmost discipline—the means to enforce a better life. Mr. Mills had written several books on enlightenment; he enlightened on issues like unquestioned loyalty and fierce admonition. It was a good thing I had my "spiritual armor" now, because Janet was in this thing deep.

And since I was lonely, and doing so "great," Janet enticed me to hang around. I was still a little raw to be back on my own, so the most comfortable choice was: *why not?*

Easily welcomed, I moved into the loft, my grip prodded to take stronger hold. And all of the young followers were so excited and happy; they practically formed a tight aisle.

Disciplined smiles and promises of *home* evoked the proposal to Janet. Only one lone voice stood outside my encirclement, the voice of a *real* friend: Al Pacino.

Shocked, Al fittingly showed up to our engagement party wearing a T-shirt. "You're getting engaged *again?*" he tried to reason, before staying just long enough for my sister Toni Jean to be starstruck.

But I was the one enamored. Even a friend's insight couldn't derail my hapless cause: a spiritual orphan believing for all things *good*. And though, deep down, I knew Al was right, I was surrounded in "in-between": a careful excursion around *wrong*.

So with full steam ahead, I bristled with emotion and pursued the available false warmth. I needed to know the source of my new radiance; it was time to meet Janet's parents.

And when I went up to the Bronx and observed Janet with her folks, I sensed a coldness, but not in reception. The estrangement was clear; the distance was kept; Janet's family existed in roles. They dutifully lived out their parts for my spectacle, while taking turns chiseling a hole drained of love.

The loft was built upon similar refuge. As I lived within this proper, courteous circle, I began to see just how tight-knit it was. The "enlightening" professed was less of inclusion and more of self-preservation. The "unknowing"—whether purposely or not—were looked at with prosecuting regard.

The group came to see me in an Off-Broadway show, and they were careful to come off "perfect" while treating the rest of the audience as inferiors. Mr. Mills had taught them that there was only one way, and they had *freed* themselves to learn well.

As an actor who liked people and mirrored the world, I questioned this infallible lesser pope. And Janet went ballistic, shredding her vocal chords in his defense, ensuring I once and for all knew the *truth.* So it was then that I saw the rabbit hole narrow, only widened to allow obsolescence. I could see that the plan was to withdraw from the world. I could see, that in this, *she* saw me.

People began to suspect me: the cook for the cult kept watching. I was considerably older than the rest of the group and was always questioning, always criticizing. On the short, sweet road to extrication, I broke it off with Janet and got my own place. But just before the group administered the provincial boot, my *other* family stepped in, albeit with *Hope.*

Bernie Barrow, the star of *Ryan's Hope,* had recommended me for the contract role of master criminal Alexei Vartova. And just like that, I was in millions of people's living rooms for six straight months.

I became recognizable—it took some getting used to. When I was out at Bloomingdale's once, I exited the elevator and heard the elevator operator say, "Wow, *he shops?*"

My recognition certainly didn't hurt prospectively either. I was offered a part in the movie *Fort Apache, The Bronx,* and I got a role in *The Recruiting Officer* at the Brooklyn Academy of Music—complete with Ann Zeigler staked out in the front row.

She really threw me for a loop during the opening number; I hadn't been expecting the past's call so soon. And while I did have sympathy, because Ann got me on the way down, I knew that forward was the only sure way.

My untested sentiment was confirmed in one of the highest compliments I ever received. Later that year when I joined *A Midsummer Night's Dream* with the BAM company, we were rehearsing and the wonderful actor Brian Murray said to me, "I have to admire the way you attack Shakespeare. You don't even know the lines yet, but you go there and you try it anyway."

And this is how I approached the cook. I didn't really know her—just that she was always looking at me. But it wasn't necessarily the hollowed ingratiation that the other cult members shared, it was more *outsider*—of my own heart—as if to say, "I'm here because I have to be."

So I stayed around the edges, attended a couple training sessions, attempted to learn all that I could. I found out she was divorced after her husband went to Leavenworth prison for objecting Vietnam. After two years of struggling, Darya had joined as a cook but was never actually part of the cult: a desperation leading to a structured assembly, a salvation found in supporting a daughter.

I started a relationship with her, becoming increasingly fond, knowing that it wouldn't be easy to take her out of the cult. At first, we rented a small house with another cult member who was "higher up"—with a gradual and careful exiting strategy of locating in Irvington, New York; they were none too inclined to leave her be.

But soon it was clear that in our time away from the loft, we had become a family. I understood that peace was within reach, and I convinced Darya of the same. She had some money from property in North Carolina, and I suggested that she absolve herself of all real estate endeavors so she could be a full-time presence in her daughter Zoe's life.

So we got an apartment in the same Westchester area and the three of us made a life for ourselves. Of course, the cult called angrily and begged for our return, but I let them know in so many words that I wouldn't hear of it. Eventually the calls quit coming, and it wasn't too much later that I forgot about the city altogether.

Life in the suburbs was completely different. Instead of the late nights, I became a morning person: I'd wake up and go for a walk. There was a beautiful private park near Main Street that we eventually moved near, and I moved away from who I once was. Darya, Zoe, and I would walk down to the playground, where I would think while we watched the setting sun.

I thought about how my father had asked me to take care of my mother and my sister, and how he put his hand on mine when I told him I would.

I thought about our relationship, and how he had denied the violin out of love. He had known the life of an artist would be hard and had only wanted the best for his son. But

I knew that at his core he must have believed, or he never would have let me off of the bus.

I thought about how he requested I sing his favorite song at his and my mother's fiftieth wedding anniversary and how I was so full of lasagna and hesitant. But Pop encouraged me because he understood the message, so I got up and sang "You'll Never Walk Alone."

On October 24, 1981, I was set to do a reading in Westchester for Vinny Gugliotti, a casting director who used to work for Joe Papp. I was playing an Italian dad, and right before I went on stage, I got the news that my father had died.

It was very hard to do the reading; but like they say, "the show must go on."

And as I was into this performance, we came upon the line where I say to the son, "You gonna be a good kid?"

And the kid said, "Yeah."

"Here's a quarter."

And the audience erupted. I realized I had said the line just like my father.

As soon as the show was over, Vinny consoled, "Dominic, thank you for doing the reading. It was wonderful. You put so much into it. I was sorry to hear about your father. I didn't know. I wouldn't have asked you to act if I'd known."

"That's all right, Vinny," I said.

Then Vinny put his hand on my chest and expressed, "You know, it's freeing in a way, sometimes. It's freeing."

And he was right. It was as though my father had let me go. When Pop died that night, something died in me too. His death was a beginning, not an ending. He had given me his blessing.

I was reborn.

Chapter 10

DARYA

Nun te scurda ca t'aggio date 'o core:
Don't forget, I gave you my heart.

Can't you see it? I know I can: a promised song for me and you. Something has happened and I want you to be there.

But I should have known they would never let her go.

And while I was singing the lyrics to this Neapolitan standard at the little Italian restaurant on New Haven's main street, a depiction of nourishment was starting to form: what I had now found could grow in this idea of "community," the acceptance awaiting the allowance of friends.

"I heard you sang 'Core 'ngrato.' Would you sing it again?"

Nicholas Pelliccio had acted upon the rumor that his Neapolitan heritage was still alive. He was a personable and well-known businessman involved in local charities, his humbleness never missing the chance to sing "A Day in the Life of a Fool." He had come in late and as I was filling in the cracks—with his support, I once again thought of "full." There were fractures in my life that I needed to explore; fortunately, in Nick, I had a friend in the oil business.

I became based; I became centered. I got involved in the Yale Repertory Theatre, also in New Haven, and Nick came to all of my performances. "My son Mark is a musician. I know what you guys are like. You never have any money," Nick would tell me; and since he owned the PESCO oil company, he wouldn't even think twice when paying for dinner after the show.

Nick introduced his whole Italian family, and Darya would come when we'd play music and have Sunday's big lunch. He encouraged my guitar, and everybody would sing, and new innocence shimmered like when I was child. Nick was even there when Mark and I decided to record "Typical New Yorker"—the song I had left unfinished when I panicked while holding Dominica; and to which I was now outstripping, letting go and becoming anything but.

My priorities were different: I cared for my soul. Darya, Zoe, and I attended the Catholic church every week, and we joined a renewal program that discussed helping others. I had spent fifty years driving toward something inward; and now, for a first, I *wanted* to give.

Music was the betterment; it guided restoration. Darya would drive me to local senior centers and nursing homes, where I would play my guitar for the wheelchair-bound; and they would sing and come to life, and resuscitate mine.

The burden was lifting; a persecution was ending: I believed I was entitled to *good*. Adapting to the domestic life, I was in *Another World*.

A yearlong contract role on the über-hit soap opera allowed me to ask two things: one, was it possible for an actor to comfortably make rent?—*yes, thanks to said contract*; and two—partly enabled by the ability to answer the first one—"What is really important in life?"

I realized that if I wanted to *give*, I had to take care of myself. I had to grow before I could really reach others—out in Irvington, this required a license.

Darya taught me to drive, at least enough to pass the test, and now I legally didn't know where I was going. Lost on the main roads in Westchester County, I searched out how I could spiritually thrive. The thirst for composure solely guided my journey, and I careened toward maturity hidden in plain sight.

Docking Pop's old Chevy at joy's nearest harbor, I commenced the healing; I made the rounds. There was the Tarrytown Nursing Center, where I was received with open hearts, and the New Rochelle Hebrew Home, where I learned humility and peace:

"I'll see you tomorrow," I'd say after playing "Hava Nagila" and other Jewish melodies.

"I hope so," the elder Mr. Jack Finkelstein would self-mockingly claim.

"I'm going to be disappointed if I don't see you," I'd add with the slightest unease.

"Not as disappointed as *I'm* gonna be," Jack commanded, breaking all fragile conditions.

Not to be outdone, the Yiddish woman followed:

"Dominic, are you a sucker?"

I figured it best to remain silent; I had no idea what to say. Perhaps this little old woman who stood at my sitting height was slightly off the rocker she might need and maybe she would just go away. She did, but returned with conviction.

"Are you a sucker??"

She had me dead to rights. "Yeah, I'm a sucker."

"Here's a candy," and she handed me a lollipop.

Many of the residents at the Hebrew Home had known people who were Holocaust survivors, some survivors themselves. I learned so much about disposition through trial—indefinite wisdom at the cost of a verse.

The music of my parents' generation was awaking youthful passions. The distant, opportunistic days with my grandparents were stirring youthful aspirations. These Americans who had come before me gave the stage to perform: they gave an artist credence for dreaming; they gave an artist a home.

And because Darya was such a spiritual person, and Irvington's arteries ran through three mansion-churches, we began to feel *part* of something. We settled in. I started to *know* the town; they knew me—even the nuns at Saint Cabrini's said, "We're always going to pray for you, Dominic." Thus, with prayers answered, small miracles ensued: the past's visit came and I reclaimed myself.

Bonk. A baby named Rose hit a baby named Sal over the head with a bottle—at least that's what I was told some sixty years later during espresso, pasta, and cookies. The retired barber now used his stubby fingers to strum: his instrument, the passion; dedication, his wife. Sal taught me new guitar chords while Rose would listen: I was back in the Bronx, and even before.

Sal's and Rose's parents had both come from Ragusa; their Sicilian home always cherished the taste. "You must meet my friend—he plays the most wonderful mandolin," Saint Cabrini's elderly resident had told me. "You two would be such a terrific duo." Surely she knew that heaven await.

The doors would open, they would be ready: it was going to be unexpected. When the elevator arrived on the floor for the hopeful, we were already playing and the residents grinned. The stocky and tall; the mandolin and guitar; Sancho Panza and Don Quixote: Sal Guastella stayed with me as we sent forth cheer—a blessing in friendship while I *quested* truth.

The light shown brighter; we sang for the skies. The residents enjoyed a bit we called "radio show"—those that were able sang as they stood. And in an effort undertook that was no small doing, I got the nice Polish woman's eight daughters to all sing at once. Their voices filled the rec room with "You Are My Sunshine"; and together, spirits lifted and soared the unknown.

Two weeks later, the nice Polish woman was dying. And I went up to her room and believed: "You've got to come back downstairs next Sunday. We're going to sing again, and you're going to sing with your daughters."

And she smiled at me, and I knew that she knew: she was happy, and she was going to die. A couple of hours later she was no longer with us, her calmness and courage still echoing on. She taught me a lot about strength and acceptance, about living life and releasing control.

I had Darya, I had Zoe, Nick, Sal, and Rose: a community I considered *my own*. I was on healthy tracks, so I didn't need the *map*; I embraced a happiness unexplored.

Then, seven years later, I drove straight to Ohio.

"Would you like to see the kids?"

I had made sure Pam always knew how to reach me.

When she called in the summer of '83 seemingly out of nowhere, I hightailed it to the Midwest as if going fast enough would get back to 1976. Alex was twelve now, and he acted shy. Dominica wouldn't let go of my hand. I spent the weekend while a family reformed; restructured, one step at a time with faith.

Everywhere I went, I was in a better *place*: there was fulfillment in family and home. Pieces were forming as I became whole; only one compromise seemed to remain.

"Dominic, what happened? You drop out of the business?"

Leave it to an actor to assume their role. But when I visited the Ensemble Studio Theatre, I knew they were right: I hadn't been rewarding my primary goal. Self-expression was in me and I needed to perform—so if I wasn't in the acting pool, there still had to be waves.

A beautiful replica existed on Main Street: Irvington had scaled down Ford's Theatre where Lincoln was shot. And it was here that I learned to stand amidst a division, that an artist's commitment to belief must be bold.

I was definitely against censorship, but I also knew the territory: we were knee-deep in the religious waters of suburban America. As a member of the local Theatre Commission, and as an actor who had once heard of this thing called "audience," I felt it was my duty to inform the board that the Immaculate Conception—the church I attended—had gotten outside word that morbid comedy *Sister Mary Ignatius Explains It All For You* was in preproduction and had sent Martin Luther himself on their behalf.

Of course, since most of the board was *fanatical* or well on their way, preproduction was dogma: selections came from above. Outnumbered, I held my ground; I stuck to my vision: I saw that we were about to take a massive swan dive. I pointed out the protest note some guy tacked to the theatre's door: I successfully defended the concept of not going belly-up.

Enthusiastically supercharged in my stand for the people, I set out to put the "community" back into a show. I wrote a play that had a little something for *everybody*—only the local Catholic priests snubbed their roles. And since my stance led to policy in prescreening works, I proudly brandished clout to thwart all would-be directors.

The production was kinetic as communal ties formed—
the arts drew involvement; I became a local leader. "One day"
thoughts of Lawrence Welk and future cabarets were born:
my director's chair the muse, crowded with emanations.
And while exultation bred ascension where I watched united
growth, a view was gained of what's important, and I saw what
lay before.

Sto'a suffri pe' chella lla:
I am suffering from such a great love.

There were more gifts than those given, and there was a
bond, and there was one thing left to do. So on my fifty-third
birthday, I stood with a friend—in my apartment, I married
Darya.

She was lovely and she always spoke softly with wisdom;
and I loved her daughter, Zoe, too. She was also "my" child,
and together we raised her, and all of my family in attendance
at the wedding approved.

I was acknowledging and searching, becoming outward
bound. So after three years of togetherness, we went to visit
Darya's family in Oregon. I had never traveled that far west,
and for the first time—in a long time—I was *wide open.*

Maybe it *was* "only chicken wire"—perhaps, and unfortunately, Dominic Jr. had been right. This thought occurred as
I slowly backed up, on Darya's parents' farm, and away from
the fence. The problem that existed, in so much as I could
tell, was that the bull could still see me.

"Look, a potato!" I reached down and exclaimed, shortly after the "typical New Yorker" was informed that cows come in black and bulls usually have horns—Darya's family was kind.

Her father ran a loose church whose Sunday playlist blasted folk tunes. Her sister, a violinist, and her husband let me lend my pipes to the bluegrass band: an essential, family affair. And when Darya's environment inspired her to retake the flute, we all sat around and played under tranquil Western skies.

I saw rodeos with *real* longhorns; I absorbed the culture of indigenous Native American tribes; I learned the legend of Multnomah Falls—the chief's daughter's leap for the common good: out of my element is where it had taken residence, a spirit reconnected, the heart I owned as a child.

New roots tore into the fertile grounds, starving at cultivation. I needed to communicate the ability to heal: Darya had been waiting to draw from the born-again well.

Irvington ground out the truth until it was small and compact: tidy, like the town itself. Rituals of the church overlaid preformed judgments, and the opinions of many became *locked down*. And whatever confinement didn't survive granulation was left to shrivel on its own. But the tide was coming—freeing waterways opened—seeking those who had remained on its shores. This is how they found her.

There was no accessible head, yet the hammer came down; rigid, nobody jumped to sing and shout. The missing excitement was guaranteed at the edge: the group's offer incarnated as a new church movement sept. *Structures were fossilized, masters couldn't be reached*; and since anyone was "welcome," Darya showed me where to dip, while she prepared to make the jump.

"In the name of…Boom!" There had been an emphasis. I didn't quite catch the name, but the fifty businessmen were right to bring in a ringer; I definitely heard the boom. The guy they selected to put his hand on me was good: it felt like an initiation.

Fairly all Italian, held by reformation glue, and affiliated with Darya's newfound spirit-filled and charismatic church, the Full Gospel Businessmen enjoyed singing while evolving the framework, changes made upon further comprehending "the" Word.

Serenity blanketed suburbia, and I would testify to that. With the gentle, all-knowing nudge of Full Gospel, local television was the means to best bring them in. Addicts would call in to call out, and I'd confess the cathedral and tell of the moment that led me to be. Ensconced with appeasement, Darya couldn't have been happier: her discovered evangelism was how we'd submerge.

But while I was willfully going under, John Lithgow was thankfully coming up. He was excellent and carried *Requiem for a Heavyweight* at New Haven's Long Wharf Theatre, leading Richard Dreyfuss and me in the standing ovations that justified a national tour. And while Richard nailed his part as Maish, he wasn't available to come—so an apt recast quickly found George Segal. On stage, I played a gangster;

in the untried seas is where I fished for *character:* the director aptly stated, "Dominic, be prepared. George is going to try something new."

Acting roles were always a challenge and rehearsal didn't end with certainty: after four or five weeks, I still wasn't sure who the part was. I knew I could deliver but would strain the dialogue at first, audience approval then permitting the real wearing of skin. I thought I had to have all of the possibilities readied; I was always in a state of *why?* Thus, a period of acclimation would evince tension and hesitation; and a lack of trust in self would run throughout.

In one scene within *Requiem for a Heavyweight,* the gangster I played approached Maish to let him know that it's time to produce "the money" or I and company had a "production" of our own. And the scene called for a moment of menacing silence before any speaking; it took a commanding walk which I knew, having performed it several times.

But unbeknownst to me, George's "something new" was a secret so precious it was never to be told, and George instantly took it all the way: on the spot, Maish dropped and begged. Of course, this changed my whole attitude toward him—it made me disgusted; my gangster lost any last shred of respect. And the oracle director, somehow unburst with eureka, took his scratchpad to the world and tastefully admonished the future of theatre: "Nah, it's not going to work."

Just as I had adjusted too: the thing was, I *had* adjusted. This time, I believed to know the role—I wasn't worrying about the outcome; I wasn't asking *why?* By releasing the doubt, I was working more organically; with newly entrusted emotions, I was learning my *character*.

We performed in the Palm Beach Playhouse, and Darya and Zoe got to see Florida; we played Dallas's Majestic Theatre too: everywhere we toured, we were packing the big houses—and the crowds were rewarding with stifling applause. So our nationally approved juggernaut rolled onward, and in March of 1985, we finally hit it big.

There were lights, there was glitz, and we already knew about the glamour: this was Broadway, and productions were grand! But apparently the gold standard didn't do it for everyone; our "unsatisfied" producer barely promoted the show. Still, with full speed ahead, we scoured the icy depths: we pressed forward with little to no advance ticket sales. We were the audience-backed champion, the titanic of acclamation, so we stayed the course as the iceberg dawned.

It was quick and it was cold, and it was over in a matter of days. Three nights in and a review took us down; we didn't even last the first week. All of the hardworking talent in a popular show gone, immediately, because some critic opined—even Richard Dreyfuss had enough belief in it to personally see it on tour. Embittered, I resented the structure: the powerful "poisons" of the unaffected few. When relaying the events to fellow EST actors, I fervidly added, "I think I'll leave the business for a while."

Who needed it anyway? I had *life* to look forward to: Darya and I were making beautiful music together, literally—she hadn't put down the flute; as troubadours-for-hire, Sal and

I branched out to colleges and weddings—livening up the party with our senior center act; and the Full Gospel Businessmen, though noticeably more organized now, still offered an open door to discuss and redefine *change*—from Darya's affectation, her group must have also been harmlessly docile.

And with this contentment, we glossily strolled into one of the first events ever attended by the new "Mr. and *Mrs.* Dominic Chianese"—proudly arriving, unaware that elbows rubbed had conspired to chafe.

I danced with the bride, and feelings were strong: she was beautiful, yet there should have been more. A season was turning—I felt I was different—but there were some things I couldn't undo.

Almost twenty years had passed, and there was no forgiveness; still enraged, Sima was patient. She had demanded Merle hide our daughter Rebecca's wedding from my mother, and Rebecca couldn't shoulder the strength to fight her fire. Damage was intended, and Toni Jean knew it, becoming extremely defensive that our mother's absence was for the infliction of pain.

And it worked, and it evidenced constructed imperfections, the repercussions—things as they really were: a "completeness" wouldn't exist without *all* of the past's entirety; and when I returned without the rose-tint, I descried ensnaring thorns.

Lined trees led to mansions in affluent Westchester County, and the highly praised schools entailed. Upon further inspection, Darya and I pulled Zoe out: the classrooms were all *three-ringed*. Accolades were tallied by newspaper fronts on behalf of circus brochures: the only thing "taught" was how everyone could float through the tests, with a bonus question of disloyalty to those who "paid rent."

In a place of acceptance, Zoe found instant success at the Dobbs Ferry Catholic School: she *studied* and received high marks. She was very musical and was great when she played Fagin in *Oliver!*—the nuns creating the atmosphere where this bright young girl could abound. And when I understood her father might be smoking pot like many of the objectors at the time, I stepped in to ensure her visits stayed "clean." I loved having children, but had not been responsible full-time; with Zoe, I could make a difference.

But while Zoe and I were becoming close, the past was holding me afar. Rebecca's wedding had indicated that the previous resounded, that forgiveness involved more than one. Dominic Jr. was aggressively into the streets; Sarah couldn't understand, she had been too young; Alex and Dominica were distantly recuperating; Lea was now long gone: removed, I reflected with a growing remorse; and in 1986, with self-decided appropriateness, I was cast as an abusive father. I never watched that particular episode of *Tales from the Darkside*; I was too busy imposed to living out the real thing.

The Full Gospel Businessmen welcomingly peddled the relieving solution: everyone comes along for the ride. The solidarity lay exclusively in the numbers, and they were now adamant with their sole answer of "one." As long as it was uncontested, everything was crystal; but my redirection of a Higher Power had been *my* experience: I couldn't even fathom telling others what to think—especially if the illumination was grey.

Fifty thousand dollars ought to clear things up. Surprisingly to me, Al Pacino and his accountant laughed. I had approached Al about expanding my dream of using art to help others, and he and his accountant wondered just how much it was that dreams cost. The nonprofit would musically reach all of the senior centers in the Northeast: by their response to my small investment conundrum, I could tell that they knew I was definitely a *dreamer.*

But Al did point me in the right direction, and I went down to the Lower East Side and obtained the rating of 501(c). The Center Stage for Seniors was in business: I asked contributors to "be a sucker"—the inspired charity slogan would have made the Yiddish woman proud. Immersed, I'd hop from one senior center to the next, organizing the shows—so richly savoring the experience I barely raised any funds. If I kept the focus on others, and I kept the music going, then I could transcend the only place where I knew that it stopped.

> Sto'a suffri pe' chella lla:
> *I'm suffering because of her.*

I was able to meet some interesting people as the wolves went after the sheep. The leader had ordered it, and I was in a relationship: I politely watched them dine. An eighty-year-old woman "*had* to accept the Lord," the new acquaintance next to me hailed. Her name was Darya, and she drew breath by *his* words, but wouldn't draw for the flute with a friend.

Her ambitions were noticeably equally minimized, trust placed in what they deemed of want. I tried to accommodate while she disengaged—as they took her, they took me apart.

And as the "voice" went out and told people how to vote, I grasped the full magnitude of this new sect: it appeared my decisions had now come to dismantle, and leave me as my former self.

Purification came in the form of a child. Zoe had a sweet sixteen party in 1988, and Rebecca brought the gift of my first grandson. And to make an amends, she carried the baby over to present him—but was forcefully blocked from my mother by a still-riling Toni Jean. Rebecca burst into tears, and my mother was speechless, and it was clear what I long ago caused. But it was also evident that Rebecca had made a first effort—that in time, perhaps, we all might go on.

In 1988, Alex also moved forward. After turning seventeen, he followed his knack for inner workings and pursued apartment contracting in greater New York. Alex immediately came up to visit, and it was wonderful to have him; and despite my transgressions, my children wanted to be near.

And if my children were finding the ways to look past, then I could work toward who I always had been. Darya's "church" and Full Gospel were straddling a fine line, so I searched for my spirit where I had become one: I returned to regional theatre. I *was* an actor.

For six months, I workshopped gangster Arnold Roth-stein in Peter Allen's *Legs Diamond,* under the direction of Bill Ackerman at the EST. Julie Wilson was featured—she was eventually nominated for a Tony—and I hoped to capture some of her magic by studying her bravado every night. Peter was also very pleasant to work with—he was fun and down-to-earth—but in a first, I was cut because I was simply too "suave." It was disappointing not to go with everyone into the Broadway version, but fortunate because it led to something possibly more.

An old friend from Brooklyn College made me an offer I couldn't refuse, but unlike with Don Corleone, I seriously tried. Joel Zwick, with whom I had performed back then, was now directing the comedy *Second Sight,* and he wanted me to play the priest. But I was resistant in my spiritual "infancy" to parody the cloth in a movie; I didn't know if a lack of rever-ence could be "counted against." However, Joel responded with a single day's work and three thousand dollars—I decided I'd figure it out.

We were filming in a cathedral up in Boston, and everyone but the AD had gone on break. And she approached me as I was in costume, tapping me on the shoulder, petitioning: "Dominic, there's a terrifying-looking man trying to get into the church, and I told him it was off-limits because we're shooting a picture. Would you please send him away? He won't leave."

She looked scared, so I decided I would talk to the intruder, and I got up to open the church's door. And the guy was standing there: tattoos up the neck, shaved head, faded leather, haunted eyes.

"Are you a father?"

And I thought, "*Well, I do have children and I am dressed like a priest...*"

"Yes, I am. Can I help you?"

"I don't know what to do. My mother just died. I need to talk to a father."

The guy really looked like he was fighting with something, so I widened the door:

"Follow me."

We were alone and he started talking about how he had been bad; I knelt before the crucifixion, and he did the same. Surrounded by candles, we prayed for a solid minute; and when I mentioned peace in his heart, he turned and it was in his face: things had now surfaced that he needed to ask; he hoped to remember; he *wanted* to cry.

Calmer, he left, and the AD reappeared; she apparently had witnessed it all.

"That was an incredible thing to do," she explained as I quietly disarmed—as an actor, as myself, as a person with a past, I had helped another human being: there was nothing I could say.

In the emotional highs and lows of a scene, dialogue is the guide. I was playing a gangster opposite Armand Assante in Sidney Lumet's *Q&A*, and my character was, refreshingly, on the *business end* of the double-cross. Sidney had us spend weeks intensely rehearsing the scene as a play, and when we were ready to film, we stripped out the "theatre physicality" and put the emphasis into the written words. It was a great technique to equip myself with: Armand and I could do the scene backwards by the time of the shoot—and it was understandable why George Segal had wanted to experiment: sincerely *wanting* new life could be a difficult thing.

Especially within the confines of family. In 1990, I also played a grief-stricken father in *The Lost Capone*, hoping his son "Al" would change. Alex had turned eighteen and drove Darya, Zoe, and me down to North Carolina for the shoot; and the fourteen-hour car ride and the movie's father and child dynamic helped me to realize my own need for family and how it was strong, and how Darya was still with me, and how the intimacy was not.

I felt very loyal; I wanted to accommodate: I respected the institutions and would *never* disappoint. When the artistic director over at Yale Rep, the great Lloyd Richards, hired me to play John of Gaunt in Shakespeare's *Richard II*, I heeded his leadership like everyone else—even when the experience put my creed to the test.

Actors were abused; Shakespeare was abused; the play's director abused his title: all could have been par at the local level, had I not passed up a lucrative TV role:

"Maybe you can get out of it." They really were making it easy.

"No, it's five days into rehearsal"—a whole five days: my devotion was *firm*.

Methinks I am a prophet new inspir'd/And thus, expiring, do foretell of him—beautiful stuff. *This royal throne of kings, this scept'red isle/ This earth of majesty, this seat of Mars/This other Eden, demi-paradise*—the director was in paradise when he wanted to hack and slash his way through this. *This blessed plot, this earth, this realm, this England*—under this direction, it sure wasn't *Kansas.*

"What happened? What happened?"

But I already knew: the bulkhead had failed to appear. What had happened was I had turned down a sublime TV appearance to work with a director who used the excuse of not being on Broadway "this time" to yell at up-and-coming actors; and now, as I was ready to make a gorgeous speech on opening night, I was being upstaged by faulty mechanics and a stage manager loud enough to be considered ad lib. What happened was that I was *furious*: they could try and foul up the rest of this cursed production, but this speech was getting delivered—*fierce.*

The next day, I saw a newspaper review that stated, "He performed the speech like he was running for Prime Minister of England." Perhaps, I had been a bit "passionate," though it ended up being a good experience: I learned to play off *all* emotions at once. And it was important that I packed that lesson into the tool kit: I was about to work with a master craftsman.

Ira Lewis's *Chinese Coffee* was a two-actor play about a writer and his mentor, and in this version, I mentored Al Pacino—but it was Al who taught me a lot. There was one scene where I lay on stage in a moment of silence, and Al would go offstage into the "kitchen"—*never* breaking character, not for one night. Shortly after his exit, I would always hear a faint tinkle of a spoon on a plate, and I realized how his imagination was always working: even offstage, his sense of truth was incredible.

Working with such a fine actor encouraged my discipline to come up to those standards. Al showed me how to efficiently rehearse in a two-character scene, employing constant emotions for four hours straight, then letting it sink in and calling it a "day": you could only cover so much ground at once, but the key was to keep covering ground. Even when we had coffee, Al stayed in the mode: "Put a little coffee in the cup," Al would say. "Take a little to keep going and then keep going." Al's work ethic and concentration motivated my own, and it was with him that I opened up and trusted to work with whole heart and soul.

And Zoe had also been zealously working. She had done so well in Catholic school that she was offered a full scholarship to the University of Scranton in Pennsylvania. I was proud of my stepdaughter for whom I was a constant presence; she had grown up and I was able to play a major role. And her pursuance of her interests came at just the right time: her parents were pursuing and were fully *absorbed.*

On February 24, 1991, I turned sixty, and most of my family was there. Rebecca and Toni Jean attended on "different sides"; Alex and my mother came; and the big surprise was that Dominica arrived—and all the photos taken proved I had a family regained. I was actually very grateful that this milestone ushered in thinning hair: it would afford the possibility to play more roles! Ages sixty to ninety were the "experienced prime," and I was becoming a full-fledged character actor.

I played a lawyer, then a judge on *Law & Order* in 1991, alongside a still supportive Michael Moriarty. When Steven Hill, who starred as the DA, offered camera-specific acting advice, Michael assured, "No, leave Dominic alone, he'll come out with it." Michael was always like that; he knew I could succeed—his assurance bolstered mine, and I knew I had grown.

Steven Seagal was also complimentary, saying he remembered me from *The Godfather: Part II* and looked forward to working together in *Out for Justice*, where much of the film's emotional crux landed on my role. I played a father whose son was "lost" to himself and the streets, and I was now able to objectively integrate the "lost sons" of my own.

Then I was cast as the villain with Joe Pesci and Barbara Hershey in *The Public Eye*, and after playing Spoleto, I was ready to fully commit to show business more than ever before.

By 1992, the Full Gospel Businessmen ran their meetings like a union: dues first, hands raised, everyone votes with "aye." It had basically become a secular town hall—the politicking wing to Darya's unmistaken cult.

Che vene a dicere stu parla ca me da:
Why do you come and say those words that hurt me so much?

219

They spoke of "the walk" but were too righteous to step: nothing was tolerated, not even the world. For over ten years, Darya and I had been together, and now she couldn't see it, and I couldn't see her.

"This is all an illusion. Real life is not here."

And that was how I knew that they got her, just like they planned.

Tutt'e passato e:
Everything is finished.

Chapter 11

MARGARET MARY

Myriads of lyrics in Neapolitan songs place the trusting heart with a woman's love. The lamenting hunt for where the model abides and sing similar reactions of: "I left my mother for you." Exaggerated examples lead to impractical results, and the songs digress into arias of pain. Thus, the Neapolitan music is accusing in that *women can hurt you*; it's "Core 'ngrato"—*Ungrateful Heart*—but it's also the last entreaty of "I need you."

The dead of winter '93 offered the warmest reception. Sarah and her husband Joe were running the Passion Place Theatre up in Woodstock, and she asked if I would be interested to play Willy Loman in *Death of a Salesman*. There would be no pay, nor any prestige, just a chance at a great role: to help my daughter. I needed a way to think things through with Darya; and in keeping with the housing traditions of rural theatres and out-of-town actors staying with available locals, when I arrived, they boarded me with Margaret Mary.

Irish, intellectual, and a pretty, light brunette, Margaret Mary was an actress who created an inviting home. And when I found out the actress playing Linda Loman couldn't go on, I suggested Margaret Mary fill in for the part: the continuation in Willy's companionship, the desolate necessitude in the staging of mine.

The production itself had a lack of direction, but I did the show regardless; I was consumed in *portrayal*: an extemporaneous peacefulness had brought security closer; a snowstorm assured I had *nowhere* to go.

"Dominic, what do you want a woman for?"

Margaret Mary was writing a book about women.

"What is the most important aspect of a woman to you?"

I could think clearly in the confines of her warm, snowed-in home, and my answer surprised her: I just wanted to be held—I wanted to *know* a woman, and know it would last; and she would know we were *there*, and we would know we were *intimate*.

Our time together in scene made us inseparable, but it was in our conversations that Margaret Mary reached my heart. She studied spirituality, so I could talk about Darya; and she played guitar, so we'd laugh and rejoice. And when we sat on the floor, listening to the radio, I could hear the yearning pangs, and I reached out for more.

In February of that year, I was set to audition for a Geena Davis film, but I couldn't leave Woodstock: I was still in the *storm*. And Margaret Mary must have wondered exactly what wouldn't lift, because she sought an answer *outside*: she opened the door.

As we walked through the woods near her house that wintery night, we intriguingly wrested where the other had been. And when I was reminded of and mentioned Leonard Cohen's song "Sisters of Mercy"—about women who were there at certain times—Margaret Mary's eyes lit up: "'Sisters of Mercy.' *That's right!*" Not only had she heard of the classic ballad, by her inference, she was *acknowledging* her role in my life.

The willing self-reference was explicitly startling; suddenly there was a distance: a fantasy exposed. Tinges of "comfort" now trailed everywhere behind me; Margaret Mary had seen them: I fell in love with "in love." I had wanted the *idea* as much as the person, and possibly compromised anything *real*. Craved attachment was safe, where I only held on to self, safely constrained to the length of the shackle; but Margaret Mary's revelation was also revolution, a reignition for the *truest*: I was free.

Chapter 12

JANE

Undefined and unrestrained, there was something I had to do. I had to relearn who I'd been in the Bronx—a repossession of the once fearless youth. To know why I fought as a teen with the mic, warding exhaustion just to somehow perform. Why it was I would stay out all night and roam, just for the chance to elicit applause: as I drove out of Woodstock, I only knew I had to get *that* back, it was my heart—*true love was still on my mind.*

The car pulled into Irvington and was home, but clearly I was not, and Darya understood. Then I informed Zoe, and Alex soon came. Harsh words were unsaid; they all helped me move.

Choosing to stay was choosing a silence, only sporadically acting—as if we were together. But the quietness still crept when gentle laughs faded away, which Darya and Zoe covered their hurt with as they walked out the door.

It was a tiny apartment: barely room for my books, my blue chair, my tears, and the *choice* to be alone. But I had written a song in transition about "hearts intertwined," about "oranges and roses"—and to this I held on.

With next to no money, I sat in the ten by seventeen studio on East 81st; and according to the neighbors, my reputation was smaller. I propositioned swapping music accompaniment for meals; but just like the home-cooked Neapolitan dishes I couldn't afford, the Italian restaurant below me just wasn't buying.

"You know, I was in *The Godfather: Part II*—maybe you would like me to sing here on the weekends," I tried at the restaurant down the block that hopefully hadn't talked to the first. "I'll work mostly for tips"—handing the owner a picture of Johnny Ola. And he didn't remember but fortunately I did: a true friendship was lasting; it never went away.

Happy to see me, Mr. O'Lunney put me on; and I'd sing, and come home to read Thomas Moore's *Care of the Soul*. Sustainment was found, then a verifying strength: my time in Irvington qualified in the book as "restored." And when I learned that—at age sixty-two—I also qualified for a pension, I brushed it aside: with new value and things to say, I *performed*.

Hushed solitude sank, providing self-examination. I spent months mostly excluded, pondering what all I'd tell. Away, my decisions actualized as *authentic*; I focused on consequences, and pulled my show off the shelf.

I recalled a time when I was artistically in charge: in Irvington, directing the inclusion of any. And to still reach the many desired, the time for action was today; piecing together an artist's id, I put together a cabaret.

And Al Pacino was becoming a one-man show too. Al won the Oscar for *Scent of a Woman* in March of 1993, and he threw a party just for his friends at a wonderful little West Village restaurant—where I came across removed about having to end things with Darya; and to uplift a friend, Al requested I sing.

Guard downed to "approachable," thanks in part to the mariachi band, Al's cousin Mark and his wife Lisa had intentions revealed: "Dominic, would you like to be in *Thérèse Raquin?* We're producing it and we need somebody to play the judge."

"No thanks."

But I was having fun now—the mariachi band was good: "But you know what I will do? I'll direct it!"

And they were happy about that—the mariachi band still good—and I spent half of that year namely…as a director.

This wasn't necessarily impressive, there were certainly the "greats," but the important thing was that it might have been impressive to *her.*

The experience was lively, Mark and Lisa indulged as the stars, and we performed in a long room with the audience just feet away and intimate. And on November 14, my friend Valerie Irwin—who I knew from O'Lunney's—came to the show, and she happened to have brought a *friend.*

Afterward, we went to O'Lunney's to celebrate, and someone had given me some roses because the play went so well; and Valerie's friend sat across the room as I sat with my song:

Two hearts intertwine/Like oranges, and roses, and bluebirds of Spring/That sing their joy whenever they sing/My dream is to share a bottle of sweet wine/Two lovers and candles and dinner for two/Reach out for me and I'll reach out for you/And though we're not touching, we know that it's true/That love can make two hearts intertwine/True love is still on my mind

So I walked over, and presented a rose; by her smile, I had met Jane Pittson.

I was working on something big.

On December 5, 1993, my cabaret debuted in the back room at Danny's Grand Sea Palace on 46th—the *heart* of the theatre district. The piano player was there, and the drummer talked himself into the mix, and we played fourteen loosely connected songs with the theme: what I wanted.

Jane came with Valerie, and my mother baked a cake, and Toni Jean and my children all showed tremendous support. Even Mr. O'Lunney stopped by—in all, about seventy people—and there had to be something *right* to feel that good in a show.

Passion was seeping—so Jane and I split a cab home, and our plans to go out for dinner were derailed by a coffee. Al Pacino called me up to see if I could cover Ben Gazzara in

Connecticut; after two months of *Chinese Coffee,* I rushed back to go slow.

She was an Englishwoman who worked for the United Nations, but I was the one who didn't think it was proper yet to hold hands. Tall and elegant, blonde hair and blue eyes, Jane spoke with a very clear diction—and I heard: *it's all right.*

Still, I proceeded cautiously, but with a knowing sense: by letting things come naturally, I could accept the unsure end.

Then taken away, I was taken further.

Sitting in my dressing room at the Pittsburgh Playhouse on October 24, 1994, I was preparing to go on for Eduardo De Filippo's *Saturday, Sunday, Monday,* when I received the devastating news: exactly thirteen years to my father's passing, my friend Raul Julia had died.

Completely shocked, I barely got through the evening: nobody knew—he had just starred in *Man of La Mancha.* He was still, as of recent, singing late into the night, celebrating in steakhouses, preceding a show. Even though Raul passed at a young fifty-four, someone at the memorial adjusted he had lived through his eighties—in Raul's life, twenty-four hours were *only* twenty-four.

"Raul, what are you doing? You really shouldn't be singing now. You should be going home," I had told him.

"Ahh, don't worry about it," as he generously *lived.* Raul brought humanity to all of his friendships; I missed my friend, and couldn't think to lose more.

Attending Jane's small dinner party on East 89th, I placed my shoes by her Murphy bed: I *wanted* us to succeed. But when we mutually agreed there was a chance that we might, Jane poked her head in my door, declaring, "There's no way we can live here!"

The British were very proper.

Admitting that Jane was probably right, I gathered my belongings: we were *staying together*. But when I carried my blue chair on my head for nine blocks, she was noticeably embarrassed: "You shouldn't do that, you know."

Jane was very British.

I became exposed to finer things.

I had always enjoyed beautiful furnishings but was constantly on the "move" or reduced financially to avocados: with Jane it was okay to make a home life a priority; her awareness of etiquette was a comfortable norm.

She had come from a twenty-year marriage that had ended in divorce, and I got to know her son Colin, who lived in Colorado—making sure to make all efforts to see my sons in New York. I eased into greater books; I strove to improve. And when I looked into the mirror, it was okay what was shown.

But not everyone was pleased with the projection. In 1995, I joined Tennessee William's *The Rose Tattoo* at Circle in the Square, filling in for the actor who was set to play the priest—assuming his preordained *strict* oppression. There was no mutual give and take between the director and myself, only the director's "take what your predecessor determined your key scene would be." And my instincts told me a priest giving up a confession should be played much "bigger," but I begrudgingly went along with it—able to stomach it *this time*.

I was too enraptured for diversion to begin with: Jane and I were making for such interesting partners. She was so reserved, and I was usually a social animal; and we were always on the lookout for where we could have fun.

One thing that I had come to observe about Jane was that she took a cool-headed approach and didn't gawk at celebrities. Of course, I needed to test to this.

Knowing the routine of the theatre world like clockwork, I was dining with Jane in a quiet Joe Allen's—most of the patrons had gone to the shows. And out of the corner of my eye, I saw a figure dash in and make for where Al Pacino usually sat, and upon confirmation, I told Jane, "Excuse me a minute." This probably had an exact meaning in higher culture: I had bought a little "unquestioned" time.

And I went over to Al and proudly championed, "Al, I want you to meet my new lady, Jane." Then he came over and said hi—smoothly into discourse without disclosure of name—and Jane's sudden conveyance of recognition sent Al away with a laugh.

"Why didn't you tell me you were going to bring Al Pacino over!?" Jane tried to keep to a whisper. I knew how she always liked to plan things out: the introduction had gone better than devised.

And because Jane worked with the UN and out of foreign countries, I finally had the opportunity to travel the world. I had been to Greenland and Rio and on international shoots, but now I could focus on cultures.

We went to England and walked along the rude coasts of Bude, and when the waves hit the rocks, I understood what Shakespeare had written in John of Gaunt's speech: "this scepter'd isle...this England." And after visiting Shakespeare's home and traversing the endless countryside, I saw from where Shakespeare drew majesty and power—and understood why true beauty inspired artists to work.

But would *I* one day be established in "the business"— with my craft reaching far through the globe? I no longer doubted my family or self; the only doubt left now was to success.

In 1996, my old friend Armand Assante was playing "the Dapper Don" in the premium channel–produced *Gotti,* and he wanted me in the film. So I met with casting and soon received their response: "Dominic doesn't look tough enough to play a gangster."

Don't hire me if I'm too tall or too short, too old or too young—but don't tell me that I have to look a certain way—this time, I was angry. Much like with *The Rose Tattoo,* I was sick of being told how to perform. I *believed* I was capable for the part; I had a gut intuition: *this time,* I *insisted* they were wrong.

I picked up the phone and relayed the news to Armand, and he also wasn't so subtly pleased.

"What the heck's going on here?" as he quickly got me into the film, and my persistence paid off because I now knew HBO.

Fortuitously thereafter, a string of film roles came my way. I was in *Love Is All There Is, If Lucy Fell, The Mouse, Night Falls On*

Manhattan—admiringly getting to work with Sidney Lumet again—and *Looking for Richard*, Al Pacino's passion project of bringing Shakespeare to schools through *Richard III*.

And as appreciative for the film work as I now was, the unthinkable had yet to happen.

"Pop, you're not going to believe who I heard from!" Dominic Jr. rushed to call and say.

"Who?"

"Lea Chianese."

My daughter, whom I hadn't known for twenty-eight years.

"Did you get her number?"

"Yes, I have her number."

"Give it to me."

I could not wait one second more.

She was in Baltimore, and married, and had two children—and had looked up Dominic Jr. thinking it was me.

A few days later we were reunited, and now I had gotten it all.

I met her husband Bill, her son Tyler who was five, and Josh, who was only two, and we were all so happy that we were together, so I told Lea, "I'll be back soon."

As soon as was possible, I returned with my mother, who couldn't control the tears as we arrived. In a hug that spoke volumes across twenty-eight years, grandmother unified with grandchild. And after several days of getting to know each other, my mother gave Lea the statue of Saint Jude, explaining, "This is the saint for hopeless causes."

Finally, there was *real* peace and I could relax with all of my wonderful children, grandchildren, and Jane. Everyone loved her and would say how happy I seemed, and how I had met a woman with whom I could *be*.

I was still working in nursing homes and considering putting together a new cabaret, when a few opportunities in television arose.

I appeared in another episode of *Law & Order* and in an episode of *Cosby* in 1997; then another potential role began to develop but required going in to "cold read."

Skimming the script, it looked like two elderly people talking—but there was a line forewarning: "We may have to kill your son." I couldn't believe it, but it had a ring of truth, and when I read for the audition, the show's creator heartfully laughed.

Finishing this inconceivability, I thanked everybody and went home. Two days later, I was called by casting. I went in to read again, thanked everyone, and left. And then I was called by the actors:

"Congratulations, Dominic, you just got the job of Uncle Junior on *The Sopranos!*"

Jane, there's something I need to tell you.

I did it.

Angels Fall
and Angels Rise

EPILOGUE

Ah yes, the *high* life: cameras flashing, surrounded by stars, filming on location, then visiting exotic locales, *The Sopranos* creator David Chase treating the accompanying cast to eat in eight-hundred-year-old restaurants: my first Emmy nomination was my guarantor—there was no question, I'd made it.

It was all so sudden; I needed somewhere to breathe. I stepped out to peace and quiet at the Plaza Athénée. The Eiffel Tower near the balcony was a beautiful escape; and when I heard a neighboring door creak, I gladly anticipated who I might find—who would let me know I'm not the only one.

A world-class cosmopolitan, the upper crust perhaps? In all likelihood, I was about to partake in luxurious mingling:

I secretly hoped that, in my new "stardom," I had reached a peer-status, and it was Sophia Loren.

A little bit of rumbling, the slightest delay: maybe royalty couldn't just *step* out the door. But when I looked over, my pretension to noblesse sank back below the Tower's spire: James Gandolfini walked onto his balcony in a bathrobe, proudly puffing his cigar.

And he noticed me, and we realized the situation: beneath the need for interlude, there was deep respect. We couldn't hold it longer than the humblest of moments; we burst open with laughter—he probably expected Sophia Loren.

As Uncle Junior, I was off to the races: I was invited to the Kentucky Derby by HBO. And while I was there, I was approached by two federal agents who handed me a "Federal Marshals" badge, stating, "Just a reminder of us." We took a few pictures and I appreciated their fandom, and all the perks a hit TV show could now afford.

None as much as the musical breakthrough. Lorraine Bracco, who was excellent as Tony Soprano's psychiatrist on *The Sopranos*, had thrown a party for her Italian father—at which, naturally, I played. And after I sang "Core 'ngrato," David Chase enquired, "What does that song mean? What is that about? What is that line about, 'Tu nun'nce pienze a stu dulore mio'?"

"It means, 'you don't understand my pain.'"

"Oh," David apprised.

A year later, he put the song into the script: Uncle Junior had beaten illness, had a few drinks, and performed—the millions who viewed the third season finale of *The Sopranos* now also knew I could sing. And when Sony Music put my name alongside Frank Sinatra, Elvis Presley, and Cecilia Bartoli on the *Sopranos* soundtrack, I felt another dream had been inadvertently attained, and I advertently flipped.

Certainly my outlook was evermore merry, and I found it interesting Uncle Junior too saw in a blur. Jane told me that David Chase had me wear glasses on *The Sopranos* to toughen my look, that my unfiltered "kind eyes" wouldn't convey the "street." So when I was acting with the nonprescription glasses, everything was bigger and with less detail—and I had to let go of many formed images, of which I'd relied.

The last time I spoke with my mother was December 2000. Her brain was gone—the cancer came at age ninety-two—and I just said, "I love you, mom." And she pushed my hand forward, about three or four times, encouraging me to the end to keep moving ahead.

She died the next day at Saint Cabrini's Nursing Home where I had often performed, telling me a truth about myself to her dying day: my mother, Angelina Chianese.

While performing with Brecht's *The Resistible Rise of Arturo Ui* in 2002, the director kept mentioning the importance of a "bridge," of how a message, sometimes, must be directly communicated—of how, in the style of Brecht, someone represents an idea. I knew my mother was saying go toward what made me happy, and now I was happy just being with Jane.

And that meant building the joy into our relationship—specifically, continuing with debunked decorum. Al Pacino was there with Jane and me—having recommended me for *The Resistible Rise of Arturo Ui*—when Paul McCartney came backstage at the end of one show.

I couldn't pass it up—the test had to continue—I said: "Paul, do me a favor, I want you to meet my woman." There was no other way to put it—time was of the essence—and I didn't know what to call her because we hadn't "moved forward."

Paul came right over to Jane and was *very* gracious; it was the only other time I saw Jane with an open mouth.

Then *my* jaw nearly hit the ground when Darya finally agreed to grant me a divorce: her idea of an irreversible holy matrimony changed when she thought I was rolling in dough. She had gone to Israel to spread an all-encompassing peace, and Zoe later admirably followed; and I agreed to pay her "back" so it would be legal—her real estate dealings had helped keep us afloat.

I couldn't wait any longer; I proposed to Jane in our kitchen; and on a Sunday in June of 2003, Jane was the most irradiant bride. I was so proud that I invited all the cast and crew from *The Sopranos*, and Jane invited her friends from England and the UN. And then I realized I had overbooked the Astor House on East 81st, and I had to bribe the guy at the door to let us all in.

Jane and I spent our honeymoon in Bermuda, and from there, there was really no bound. We went to Italy and Spain, frequented London and southern France: our romance took us to all the right spots.

I am ever so grateful for everything being on *The Sopranos* has provided, including working with such immensely gifted actors, writers, and crews—and was especially saddened at the untimeliness of James. An esteemed colleague, Jimmy was like a homemade wine: you always knew you were going to enjoy him. He was an incredible actor and always very generous, and there are certain people you really love—at his memorial in Park Ridge, New Jersey, they appropriately dedicated a street to him: the "James Gandolfini Way."

Now, I'm pursuing the artist's way, welcoming the potential to broaden into music and new roles. I got to try out a sophisticate with the stunning Neve Campbell in *When Will I Be Loved* and have been able to try different parts in *The Good Wife*, *Damages*, and *Boardwalk Empire*.

I've fronted different bands, cut an album with legendary producer Dub Cornett, and played the Grand Ole Opry—leaving teary-eyed upon telling the audience my grandfather's influence in song.

And I've been able to use recognition to bring attention to other causes, such as my charity, which evolved into the Joy Through Art Foundation, and to which I was awarded the Touro College's Dean's Medal for "outstanding commitment to community" during the "With Liberty & Justice For All" dinner celebration; and to contribute to the continuation and advancement of indispensable ideas, such as positive, holistic immigration contributions, being an Ellis

Island Medal of Honor recipient amongst my other fellow Americans for "exemplifying outstanding qualities in both personal and professional life, while preserving the richness of a particular heritage."

It's good when you don't forget where you came from: we've got a thing we try and do on the Upper East Side. Coretta's sang there since the beginning—she's a ninety-five-year-old pistol! And "Candy" Candido—from around—helped lay the crooning foundation too. And now I've got my guitar, and we've been joined by many, and we all sit near the Elvis statue in Conte's grocery and jam.

But if there's one thing that I'm most thankful for in this journey, it's that my children were strong enough until I could ably *provide*. My biggest reward is that I can now help them, and that they moved past the pain as I moved past my own.

I can't express how fortunate I was, and am, to have a great family and friends. They gave me encouragement, meals, clothes, and love; they showed that it wasn't the end. I'm forever thankful for all situations where I saw another human being shine, because I know underneath what at the time I thought rough, I was developing and was refined.

Each day is for giving just a bit of what's got; I was blessed I was given the opportunity to learn.

And I can especially look back at certain people in my life and see the close guidance of steps. Whether it was Merle, who is now a practicing psychoanalyst, and of whom I am now a good friend; or Pam, who later approached me about an "owed 180k," and then sold a fabricated story for much less; or Tzippy, whom I thought of—and still correspond— as a tear formed when I sang at the YM-YWHA: the Israeli national anthem, "Hatikvah," means "the hope"; but when the residents stood and joined, I knew it meant hope for *all.*

Every decision was weighed by their presence, a path determined by a longing of love. In their assistance or in their resentment, their blessing was in leading me to the compassionately *real*: I was always *in hands*, where I'd go always *known*, and I never would have done it without these Twelve Angels.